Summer Success® Math

Patsy F. Kanter • Esta T. Elizondo • Carol Hankins

GReaT SouRCe®
EDUCATION GROUP
A Houghton Mifflin Company

NUMBER SENSE

Choose the best answer or write a response for each question.

1. What is the value of the digit 8 in 5.08?

- (A) 8 tens
- (B) 8 tenths
- (C) 8 hundreds
- (D) 8 hundredths

2. Which diagram shows $\frac{1}{4}$?

(A)

(B)

(C)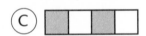

(D)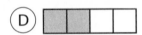

3. Which number shows 22 hundreds 1 ten 7 ones in standard form?

- (A) 220,107
- (B) 220,017
- (C) 2,217
- (D) 217

4. Which decimal and fraction describes the shaded part of the model below?

- (A) 53 and $\frac{53}{100}$
- (B) 0.53 and $\frac{53}{100}$
- (C) 47 and $\frac{47}{100}$
- (D) 0.47 and $\frac{47}{100}$

5. Which group of numbers is in order from **least** to **greatest**?

- (A) 62.00   0.620   6.200   0.062
- (B) 62.00   6.200   0.620   0.062
- (C) 0.062   0.620   6.200   62.00
- (D) 6.200   0.062   62.00   0.620

6. Which number has a 6 in the hundred thousands place?

- (A) 3,483,621
- (B) 3,683,421
- (C) 4,383,621
- (D) 6,383,421

Score: Circle the number of correct responses out of 6 items in this section.   1   2   3   4   5   6

BASIC OPERATIONS

7. Subtract.

$806
−$178

(A) $984

(B) $738

(C) $728

(D) Not Given

8. Add.

26.18
+ 47.95

(A) 73.13

(B) 74.03

(C) 74.13

(D) 64.13

9. Multiply.

36
×24

(A) 216

(B) 764

(C) 744

(D) 864

10. Complete the quotient.

$57 \div 7 = 8 R$ ___

(A) 1

(B) 2

(C) 3

(D) 4

11. Which number completes the fact family?

$3 \times 7 =$ ___ so ___ $\div 3 = 7$

(A) 10

(B) 14

(C) 21

(D) Not Given

12. Which pair of numbers rounds to 1,000?

(A) 1,081 and 1,801

(B) 1,328 and 1,088

(C) 1,489 and 427

(D) 1,701 and 659

Score: Circle the number of correct responses out of 6 items in this section.   1   2   3   4   5   6

GEOMETRY AND MEASUREMENT

13. Which word best describes the triangle?

- (A) isosceles
- (B) equilateral
- (C) scalene
- (D) obtuse

14. What is the perimeter of the rectangle?

- (A) 10 feet
- (B) 20 feet
- (C) 60 feet
- (D) 80 feet

15. What is a reasonable estimate for the length of your math textbook?

- (A) about 12 inches
- (B) about 12 feet
- (C) about 12 yards
- (D) about 12 miles

16. Choose the best unit to measure the weight of a truck.

- (A) ounce
- (B) pound
- (C) ton
- (D) inch

17. What time will it be two hours from the time shown on the clock?

- (A) 4:30
- (B) 3:30
- (C) 2:30
- (D) 1:30

18. Grace has 2 quarters, 2 dimes, and 3 nickels. How much money does she have?

- (A) $0.75
- (B) $0.80
- (C) $0.85
- (D) $0.95

Score: Circle the number of correct responses out of 6 items in this section.   1   2   3   4   5   6

PATTERNS AND ALGEBRAIC REASONING

19. Look at the number pattern.

250 300 350 400 ____

What is the missing number?

A) 400

B) 450

C) 500

D) Not Given

20. Complete the sentence.

When you multiply any number by 1, the product is always . . .

A) less than that number.

B) greater than that number.

C) equal to 1.

D) equal to that number.

21. Which number completes the equation?

$$9 \times \underline{\quad} = 54$$

A) 4

B) 5

C) 6

D) 7

22. Complete the equation.

$$46 \div 7 = \underline{\quad} \text{ R} \underline{\quad}$$

A) 6 R 4

B) 5 R 4

C) 4 R 6

D) 4 R 5

Use the grid to answer questions 23–24.

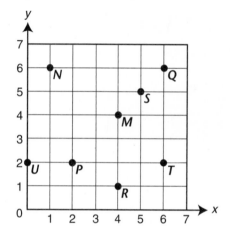

23. Name the ordered pair for Point *T*.

A) (2, 2)

B) (2, 6)

C) (6, 2)

D) (6, 6)

24. Name the point on the grid with the ordered pair (6, 1).

A) Point *N*

B) Point *Q*

C) Point *R*

D) Not Given

Score: Circle the number of correct responses out of 6 items in this section.   1   2   3   4   5   6

PROBLEM SOLVING AND DATA ANALYSIS

25. Four students are rollerblading down the path. Ella is behind Boris. Daniel is in front of Boris, but behind Leah. Who is first in line?

Ⓐ Ella

Ⓑ Boris

Ⓒ Daniel

Ⓓ Leah

26. Use the pictograph.

Favorite Sport	
Soccer	♡♡♡♡♡
Baseball	♡♡♡♡
Swimming	♡♡♡♡♡♡

KEY: ♡ = 1 student

Which sport had 1 more vote than baseball?

Ⓐ Soccer

Ⓑ Baseball

Ⓒ Swimming

Ⓓ Not Given

27. You reach into a bag with 7 red marbles and 2 black marbles. Which marble are you more likely to pull out? Why do you think so?

Answer: _____

Use the table to answer questions 28–29.

Getting to School

Method	Number of Students
Walk	2
Car	8
School bus	9
Bike	3

28. How many students are driven to school by car?

Ⓐ 3

Ⓑ 8

Ⓒ 17

Ⓓ 19

29. Suppose a new student joins the class. That student is driven to school by car. How would the data in the table change?

Answer: _____

_____

30. You pull 2 shapes from the bag without looking. Which combination is a possible outcome?

Ⓐ

Ⓑ ◯ ◯

Ⓒ ☆ ☆

Ⓓ ⬭ ⬭

Score: Circle the number of correct responses out of 6 items in this section.   1   2   3   4   5   6

Today's Number: 1

Name _____

For questions 1–6, complete only those problems using whole numbers.

1. $\frac{1}{2} + \frac{1}{2} =$ _____

2. $9{,}999 + 1 =$ _____

3. $1000 \times 1 =$ _____

4. $100 - 1 =$ _____

5. $10 \times 1 =$ _____

6. $1 + 1 + 1 + 1 = 1 \times$ _____

Write each number in standard form.
In the next space, write the number that is one more.

7. one thousand, seven hundred ten _____ _____

8. twelve thousand, six hundred fifty-three _____ _____

9. four hundred one _____ _____

10. eleven thousand, eleven _____ _____

Continue each pattern. Then tell what you did.

11. 10, 100, 1000, _____, _____

_____

12. 100, 200, 300, _____, _____

_____

13. 150, 200, 250, _____, _____

_____

14. 11, 21, 31, _____, _____, _____

_____

DRAW

WRITE

_____
_____
_____
_____
_____
_____
_____
_____

2–7

For questions 1–6, complete only those problems using whole numbers.

1. $\frac{1}{4} + \frac{1}{4} =$ _____

2. $19{,}999 + 1 =$ _____

3. two hundreds + twelve tens + twenty ones = _____

4. $22.12 - 10.02 =$ _____

5. $10 \times 2 =$ _____

82–83

6. $2 \times 6 =$ _____ so _____ $\div 2 = 6$

90

Circle all the multiples of 2.

7. 1   2   3   4   5   6   7   8   9   10   11   12

82–83

Write the fact family for each array.

8.  _____

9. _____

10. _____

11. _____

DRAW

WRITE

_____

_____

_____

_____

_____

_____

_____

_____

Money in the Pocket

Subtraction Action

◆ **MATERIALS**

2 sets of 0–9 Digit Cards cardstock (20 cards), 5 Counters cardstock, paper, pencil

◆ **DIRECTIONS**

1. Players make a recording sheet like the one shown below.

2. Each player shuffles a set of Digit Cards and spreads them out facedown on the table.

3. Players each turn over five Digit Cards and arrange them into a 2-digit subtraction problem that will yield the greatest difference.

4. Players discard the Digit Card that seems least helpful.

5. Players compute their differences on the recording sheet and compare their answers. The player with the greatest difference wins the round and receives one counter.

6. After five rounds, the player with the most counters is the winner.

	Subtraction Problem	Difference
Round 1		
Round 2		
Round 3		
Round 4		
Round 5		

Today's Number:

3

Name _____

82–83 **For questions 1–4, complete only those problems using whole numbers.**

1. $3 \times 3 =$ _____ so _____ $\div 3 = 3$ 2. $3 \times 4 =$ _____ so _____ $\div 3 = 4$

3. $3 \times 5 =$ _____ so _____ $\div 3 = 5$ 4. $3 \times 6 =$ _____ so _____ $\div 3 = 6$

2–9 **Write each number in standard form.**

5. three hundred seven _____

6. three thousand, sixty-eight _____

7. three hundred forty-three _____

8. thirty thousand, five hundred ten _____

335–339 **Use the clock to answer questions 9–13.**

9. What time will it be three hours
   from the time shown on the clock? _____

10. What time was it four and one-half hours ago? _____

11. How many minutes until it will be 4:15? _____

12. What might you be doing at 3:00 A.M.? _____

13. What might you be doing at 3:00 P.M.? _____

DRAW

WRITE

_____

_____

_____

_____

_____

_____

_____

_____

Today's Number:

4

Name _____

129–130

Round each number to the nearest 10, 100, and 1000.
Complete only those problems using whole numbers.

1. 144 _____, _____, _____

2. 4234 _____, _____, _____

3. 6578 _____, _____, _____

4. 412.22 _____, _____, _____

362–363

There are 100 centimeters in one meter. Use this fact to answer questions 5–8.

5. 4 meters = _____ centimeters

6. 8 meters = _____ centimeters

7. 16 meters = _____ centimeters

8. 700 centimeters = _____ meters

328–329

Circle the items below that have the shape of a cone.

9.

61

Solve the problem.

10. A teacher wants to arrange 12 students into equal rows.
How many ways can the teacher arrange the students? _____
Draw arrays to illustrate your answer.

DRAW

WRITE

_____

_____

_____

_____

_____

_____

_____

_____

Centimeter Ruler

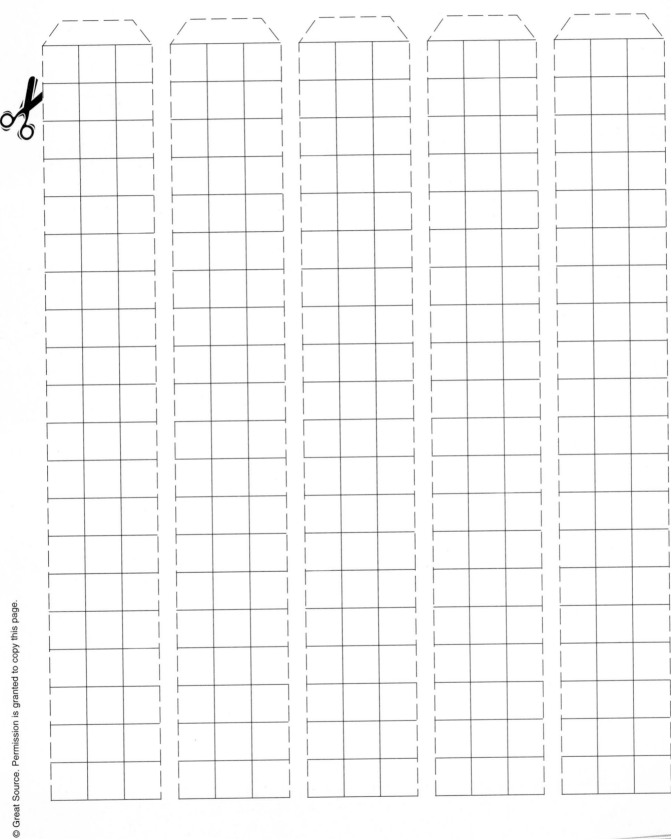

Centimeter Strips

Making Big Numbers

MATERIALS

2 sets of 0–9 Digit Cards cardstock (20 cards), 5 Counters cardstock, paper, pencil

DIRECTIONS

1. Each player makes a recording sheet like the one shown below.

2. Each player uses one set of 0–9 Digit Cards. Shuffle the cards and place them in a stack facedown on the table.

3. Player 1 turns over the top card, records the number on that card in any one of the place value columns on the recording sheet, and places the card in a discard pile. Player 2 turns over the top card, records the number in the same way, and places the card in a discard pile.

4. Players alternate turns until each player has created a 4-digit number. Numbers must be recorded before the next card is drawn and cannot be changed once they are written.

5. Players record a number sentence comparing their number to the other player's number. The math symbols <, >, and = should be used.

6. The player with the larger number receives a counter.

7. After five rounds, the player with more counters is the winner.

	Thousands Place	Hundreds Place	Tens Place	Ones Place	Comparison Number Sentence
Example:	4000 +	900 +	70 +	8+	4978 < 6784
Round 1					
Round 2					
Round 3					
Round 4					
Round 5					

Today's Number: 5

Name _____

146–152
159–167

Add or subtract. Complete only those problems using whole numbers.

1. 568 − 271 = _____

2. 374 − 299 = _____

3. 177.55 − 106.72 = _____

4. 841 + 349 = _____

5. 45.20 + 15.11 = _____

6. 694 + 281 = _____

7. 127 + 376 = _____

8. 864 − 125 = _____

9. $\frac{4}{5} - \frac{1}{5}$ = _____

10. 217 − 132 = _____

12

Compare the sums and products. Write <, >, or =.

11. 5 + 10 + 15 _____ 5 × 4

12. 10 + 5 + 5 _____ 5 + 5 + 3 + 2 + 3 + 2

13. (5 × 2) + 3 _____ 5 × (2 + 3)

14. 5 × 8 _____ 8 × 5

369–384

Solve the problem.

15. Joan is making beaded necklaces for her 5 friends. She has
2 hours to make the necklaces. If she needs 8 pieces of string
for each necklace, how many pieces of string will Joan use? _____

DRAW

WRITE

Recording Sheet

Estimated Length	Items at School	Actual Length of Item	Difference Between Estimated Length and Actual Length
1. 10 cm	_____	_____	_____
2. 20 cm	_____	_____	_____
3. 50 cm	_____	_____	_____
4. 1 meter	_____	_____	_____

Estimated Length	Items at Home	Actual Length of Item	Difference Between Estimated Length and Actual Length
1. 10 cm	_____	_____	_____
2. 20 cm	_____	_____	_____
3. 50 cm	_____	_____	_____
4. 1 meter	_____	_____	_____

Family Member's Name	Height
_____	_____
_____	_____
_____	_____
_____	_____

List the members of your family in order from shortest to tallest.

_____

_____

Weekly Newsletter

Each week your child will be bringing home Make & Take activities that have been made and used in class. These activities will provide you with materials to help your child explore mathematical concepts. For additional hints, definitions, or explanations refer to the *Math to Know** handbook pages listed below each activity title.

This week your child made a game called **Money in the Pocket**. Players practice place value by creating the largest possible numbers and trading different denominations of play money.

MONEY IN THE POCKET

Place Value: 2–7

1. The object of the game is to be the first player to get as close to $10,000 in the place value pockets without going over.

2. Players take turns tossing the 1–6 number cube and deciding whether to take that number of ten-, hundred-, or thousand-dollar bills. The bills are inserted into the correct pocket on the place value mat.

3. Players record the result of each toss on the recording sheet.

4. Whenever possible, players trade for the next-higher value bill.

Play the game several times so that you have time to observe and assess your child's skills.

- Does your child demonstrate number sense in creating the largest number?

- Does your child trade the correct amount of money for the next highest denomination?

- Can your child read four-digit numbers correctly and easily?

The directions for Money in the Pocket call for the use of a 1–6 number cube. If that is not available, use small sheets of paper with the numbers 1 through 6 written on them and put them in a paper bag. Players draw a card from the bag to determine how many play money bills to take.

Next, you and your child have an opportunity to sharpen measurement skills while working with the **Centimeter Ruler**. This activity comes with a Recording Sheet that requires your child to make predictions and actual measurements of items around the house, including family members!

CENTIMETER RULER

Metric Length: 347

1. Have your child find objects at home that he or she estimates to be 10 cm, 20 cm, 50 cm, and 1 meter long.

2. Your child should then measure the items with the Centimeter Ruler.

3. On the Recording Sheet, have your child write the names of the items and the actual lengths of the items. Then he or she should calculate and record the difference between the estimated length and the actual length of each item.

4. Have your child use the Centimeter Ruler to measure the height of each person in your family. She or he should write the measurements on the Recording Sheet and list the heights of the family members in order from shortest to tallest.

Enjoy these activities with your child and remember that the more your child engages in hands-on practice, the more her or his math skills will develop.

Math to Know is a mathematics handbook published by Great Source Education Group. For information on ordering *Math to Know* call 800-289-4490 or visit www.greatsource.com.

PRACTICE

Today's Number: 6

Name _____

91, 256–257

For questions 1–6, complete only those problems with even numbers on the right side of the equal signs.

1. 6 + 3 + _____ = 16
2. 6 × _____ = 42
3. 6 + 6 + 5 + _____ = 21

4. 6 × _____ = 54
5. 48 ÷ _____ = 6
6. (6 × _____) + 2 = 20

18–19

Make each of the following amounts using six coins.

7. 76 cents _____

8. 87 cents _____

9. 66 cents _____

10. 24 cents _____

346

Circle the items in this list that are more than one foot long.

11. A piece of chalk   A football field   A paper clip   A computer keyboard

60–61

Solve the problem.

12. There are 6 stickers on a sheet and 12 stickers in a package.
    Erin buys 4 sheets and Daneesha buys 2 packages.
    How many stickers does each of them have?

    _____

DRAW

WRITE

_____

_____

_____

_____

_____

_____

_____

_____

Exploring Shapes

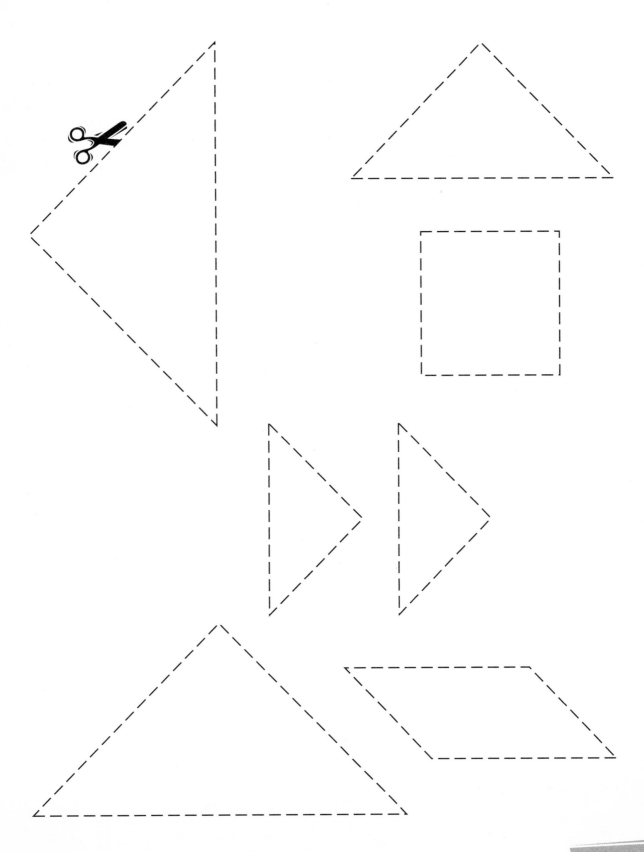

Shape Pieces

Find the Factors

MATERIALS

2 sets of 0–9 Digit Cards cardstock (20 cards), paper, pencil

DIRECTIONS

1. Players make a recording sheet like the one shown below. Shuffle the Digit Cards and place them in a stack facedown on the table.

2. Player 1 picks up the top card but does not show it.

3. Player 2 turns over the next card and places it faceup on the table. If the card is a zero, it is placed back in the stack and the next card is turned over.

4. Player 1 multiplies the number on his or her hidden card by the number on the faceup card and states the product.

5. Player 2 must guess the hidden factor that is on Player 1's card and write the multiplication fact family for that set of facts on the recording sheet. If correct, Player 2 gets both cards. If the guess and/or the fact family is not correct, the cards are returned to the deck. The cards should be shuffled after each round.

6. Players alternate turns until there are no cards left in the stack.

7. At the end of play, the player with the most cards is the winner.

	Factor	Product	Hidden Factor	Fact Family	
Example:	8	56	7	$8 \times 7 = 56$	$7 \times 8 = 56$
				$56 \div 7 = 8$	$56 \div 8 = 7$

91, 185

For questions 1–6, complete only problems with answers that are odd numbers.

1. 24 ÷ 7 = _____ R _____

2. (7 × _____) + 3 = 24

3. 54 ÷ 7 = _____ R _____

4. (7 × _____) + 5 = 54

5. 44 ÷ 7 = _____ R _____

6. (7 × _____) + 2 = 44

348

Find the perimeter of each shape.

7.
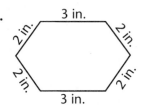
3 in.
2 in.
2 in.
2 in.
2 in.
3 in.

8.
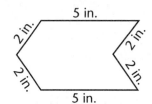
5 in.
2 in.
2 in.
2 in.
2 in.
5 in.

9.
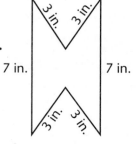
3 in.
3 in.
7 in.
7 in.
3 in.
3 in.

perimeter: _____

perimeter: _____

perimeter: _____

338–339

Solve the problem.

10. Pablo got on the bus at 7:45. He traveled 1 hour and 27 minutes to the next town. Rosario met him there and they traveled 42 minutes to the next town. How much time did Pablo spend traveling on the bus? _____

11. Explain how you got your answer._____

_____

DRAW

WRITE

_____

_____

_____

_____

_____

_____

_____

_____

91, 146–152

For questions 1–5, complete only problems with answers that are even numbers.

1.	4788	2.	8642	3.	9889	4.	2375	5.	3093
	+ 8837		+ 7412		+ 6569		+ 5429		+ 4179

6. In the above problems, how can you tell which ones will have answers that are even numbers without solving the entire problem?

_____

5–11

Write each number in expanded form.

7. 84,698 _____

8. 62,593 _____

9. 108,731 _____

10. 347,025 _____

212–213

Draw a square and shade one-fourth of it.

11.

DRAW

WRITE

_____
_____
_____
_____
_____
_____
_____
_____

Subtraction Action Variation

◆ MATERIALS

2 sets of 0–9 Digit Cards cardstock (20 cards), 5 Counters cardstock, paper, pencil

◆ DIRECTIONS

1. Make a recording sheet like the one shown below.

2. Each player shuffles a set of Digit Cards (10 cards) and places them facedown on the table.

3. Players each turn over seven of their ten Digit Cards and arrange them into a 3-digit subtraction problem that will yield the smallest difference. Zero cannot be used in the hundreds place.

4. Players discard the Digit Card that seems least helpful.

5. Players compute the differences on the recording sheet and compare their answers.

6. The player with the smallest difference wins the round and receives a counter. The next round begins after all the cards have been reshuffled.

7. After five rounds, the player with the most counters is the winner.

Player 1	Player 2
1.	1.
2.	2.
3.	3.
4.	4.
5.	5.
Strategies that I used	Strategies that I used

Round each number to the nearest 10, 100, and 1000.
Complete only those problems with answers that are even numbers.

1. 9999 _____ _____ _____

2. 829 _____ _____ _____

3. 551 _____ _____ _____

4. 427 _____ _____ _____

5. 125 _____ _____ _____

Order the numbers from least to greatest.

6. 525, 255, 552, 252 _____

7. 316, 163, 166, 306 _____

8. 101, 110, 100, 111 _____

Solve the problem.

9. Anna can type 90 words per minute.
How many words can she type in 9 hours? _____

10. What strategy did you use to solve the problem? _____
_____

DRAW

WRITE

_____
_____
_____
_____
_____
_____
_____
_____

91, 120

For questions 1–5, complete only problems with answers that are even numbers.

1. $1 \times 10 =$ _____ $1 \times 100 =$ _____ $1 \times 1000 =$ _____

2. $2 \times 10 =$ _____ $2 \times 100 =$ _____ $2 \times 1000 =$ _____

3. $5 \times 10 =$ _____ $5 \times 100 =$ _____ $5 \times 1000 =$ _____

4. $15 \times 10 =$ _____ $15 \times 100 =$ _____ $15 \times 1000 =$ _____

5. $40 \times 70 =$ _____ $40 \times 700 =$ _____ $40 \times 7000 =$ _____

5–8

Write each number in standard form.

6. 15 hundreds, 14 tens, 13 ones _____

7. 22 hundreds, 12 tens, 16 ones _____

8. 2 thousands, 7 hundreds, 11 tens, 18 ones _____

374–375

Continue the pattern.

9. , , , , , , _____ , _____ ,

DRAW

WRITE

_____
_____
_____
_____
_____
_____
_____
_____

Weekly Newsletter

Please find this week's Newsletter on page 91.

29 Order each set of numbers from least to greatest.

1. 11.0, 1.10, 0.11, 1.01 _____

2. 0.97, 0.09, 0.79, 0.07 _____

3. 4.01, 0.41, 4.10, 0.14 _____

131 Round each decimal to the nearest whole number.

4. 9.45 _____   5. 11.21 _____   6. 7.65 _____   7. 19.77 _____

358 Choose the best unit of weight to measure each item. Write oz, lb, or T.

8. A paper clip _____   9. A large dog _____

10. A car _____   11. A butterfly _____

Solve the problems.

392–393 12. Lorena has 11 one-dollar bills, 11 quarters, 8 dimes, and 6 nickels. She wants to buy a game that costs $17.85. How much more money does she need? _____

396–397 13. Four students are standing in line. Don is standing behind Kris. Pam is standing in front of Kris, but behind Yuko. From first to last, in what order are the students standing?

_____

DRAW

WRITE

_____
_____
_____
_____
_____
_____
_____
_____

X	1	2	3	4	5
1					
2					
3					
4					
5					

Fraction/Decimal Match-Up

MATERIALS

1 set of Fraction/Decimal Cards I cardstock (20 cards) and 1 set of Fraction/Decimal Cards II cardstock (20 cards)

DIRECTIONS

1. Shuffle the cards and place them facedown on the table.

2. Player 1 turns over the top two cards, reads them aloud, and compares them. If the two cards match in value, the player keeps both cards. Matches may be fraction to fraction, decimal to decimal, or fraction to decimal. If the two cards do not match in value, the cards are placed back into the facedown stack, which is reshuffled.

3. Player 2 repeats the same steps.

4. Play alternates back and forth until the facedown stack is depleted and all the cards have been matched.

5. Both players then arrange their cards in order from least to greatest on the table in front of them.

6. The player with the most matches and who has her or his cards in the correct order is the winner. If a player thinks the winner's cards are not in the correct order, he or she can challenge the winner. If an error has been made in the winner's lineup, the player who made the challenge becomes the winner.

I have 0.80 and $\frac{8}{10}$ They match, so I can keep both cards.

Today's Number: **12**

Name _____

27–28 Use <, >, or = to compare the numbers.

1. 12.1 ____ 12.01   2. 0.12 ____ 1.02   3. 0.1 ____ 0.10

4. 0.21 ____ 0.20   5. 12.20 ____ 12.02   6. 0.2 ____ 0.25

174 Find each product.

7. 42   8. 14   9. 18   10. 24
   × 12   × 36   × 28   × 21

11. What do you notice about the products of these problems?

_____

350–352 Find the area of each rectangle.

12.
    3 in.

    4 in.   Area = _____

13. 12 cm

    3 cm

    Area = _____

118–121 Use mental math to find each product.

14. 12 × 10 = _____   15. 12 × 100 = _____   16. 12 × 1000 = _____

17. 12 × 12 = _____   18. 120 × 120 = _____   19. 12 × 1200 = _____

DRAW

WRITE

Today's Number:
13

Name _____

Write a fraction and a decimal for each shaded part.

30

1.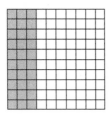

2.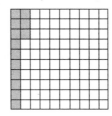

3.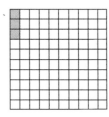

_____   _____   _____

Write each number in expanded form.

5–10

4. 13,675 _____

5. 125,303 _____

Use the table to solve the problems.

268

6. How many boys are enrolled in grades 3–6? _____

7. How many girls are enrolled in grades 3–6? _____

8. How many students are enrolled in grades 3–6? _____

Howe School Enrollment

Grade	Girls	Boys
3	67	53
4	74	81
5	87	95
6	93	80

9. Which grade has the most students enrolled? _____

10. Which grade has the fewest students enrolled? _____

DRAW

WRITE

_____
_____
_____
_____
_____
_____
_____
_____

Multiply to Make 100

1 2 3 4 5

6 7 8 9

1 2 3 4 5

6 7 8 9

Expanding Big Numbers

◆ MATERIALS

2 sets of 0–9 Digit Cards cardstock (20 cards), 10 Counters cardstock, paper, pencils

◆ DIRECTIONS

1. Each player makes a recording sheet like the one shown below.

2. Each player shuffles one set of 0–9 Digit Cards and places them facedown on the table.

3. Both players draw one card from their stacks and record the number in one of the five place value columns on their recording sheets. The correct number of zeroes should be added to the number. For example, if a 9 is drawn and used in the hundreds place, the number 900 should be written in the hundreds column. Once the number has been written, no changes are allowed.

4. Both players draw a second card and repeat the steps described. Play continues until both players have created five-digit numbers written in expanded form.

5. Players write a number sentence comparing the two five-digit numbers that have been created. The math symbols < and > should be used.

6. The player with the larger number receives a counter.

7. After five rounds, the player with more counters is the winner.

	Ten Thousands Place	Thousands Place	Hundreds Place	Tens Place	Ones Place	Comparison Number Sentence
Example:	10,000 +	4,000 +	900 +	70 +	8 +	14,978 < 16,784
Round 1						
Round 2						
Round 3						
Round 4						
Round 5						

Today's Number: **14**

Name _____

171

For questions 1–4, solve only those problems with decimals.

1. 14
    × 24

2. $14.73
    − $12.22

3. $114.73
    − $112.22

4. $514.73
    − $512.22

291–293

Use words from the word bank to describe the probability of spinning white on each spinner.

Word Bank: impossible   certain   likely   equally likely   unlikely

5.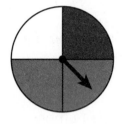

6.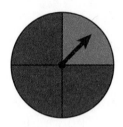

7.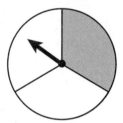

_____   _____   _____

8.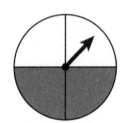

9.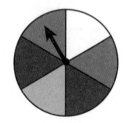

10.

_____   _____   _____

DRAW

WRITE

_____
_____
_____
_____
_____
_____
_____
_____

Round each number to the nearest thousand. Solve only problems with decimals.

131

1. 1525.15 _____

2. 1252.25 _____

3. 4552.52 _____

4. 15,255 _____

5. 12,252.55 _____

6. 22,525 _____

Use the calendar to solve the problems.

341

MAY

SUN.	MON.	TUES.	WED.	THURS.	FRI.	SAT.
				1	2	3	4
5	6	7	8	9	10	11
12	13	14	15	16	17	18
19	20	21	22	23	24	25
26	27	28	29	30	31	

7. How many Tuesdays are in the month? _____

8. What day is the 15th day of the month? _____

9. What day of the week is one week after May 10th? _____

10. What will be the date eight days after May 16th? _____

11. What will be the date one week from May 25th? _____

Solve the problems.

291–293

Ted reaches into a bag that has 5 red crayons and 7 blue crayons.

12. Which color crayon is Ted most likely to draw? _____ Why do you think so?

_____

13. What color crayon would be impossible for Ted to draw? _____

DRAW

WRITE

_____

_____

_____

_____

_____

_____

_____

_____

_____

Weekly Newsletter

Each week your child will be bringing home Make & Take activities that have been made and used in class. These activities will provide you with materials to help your child explore mathematical concepts. For additional hints, definitions, or explanations refer to the *Math to Know* handbook pages listed below each activity title.

It will be fun for your child to practice multiplication facts by playing 5 x 5 **Cover-Up** at home.

5 X 5 COVER-UP

Multiplication Fact Strategies: 66–73

1. Each player uses 9 counters of the same color. The object is to get 4 counters in one row or column on the Multiplication Table.

2. Players take turns rolling the number cubes and determining the product of the factors showing. The number 6 is used as a "Wild Number." When a 6 is rolled, the player may choose to use any number 1 through 5 as a factor.

3. Players decide where to place their counters on the Multiplication Table. For example, if 3 and 4 are rolled, decide whether to place the counter on the product for 3 x 4 or 4 x 3. For each counter placed, the player must say the complete multiplication fact.

4. The first player to get 4 counters in one row or column is the winner.

Playing **Multiply to Make 100** at home will help your child become more familiar with both addition and multiplication.

MULTIPLY TO MAKE 100

Multiplication Fact Strategies: 66–73
Adding Whole Numbers: 146–153

1. Each player should make a recording sheet like the one shown. The object of the game is to have the sum closest to 100 without going over.

2. The 1–9 Digit Cards are shuffled and placed facedown on the table.

3. Player 1 draws 6 cards from the top of the stack. He or she arranges 4 of the cards into two multiplication problems that will yield the greatest products. For example, if 1, 2, 3, 7, 8, and 9 are drawn, the largest products can be made using 3, 7, 8, and 9. The remaining two cards are set aside.

4. Player 1 records the chosen digits on the recording sheet. Then that player writes and solves the two multiplication problems. Finally, the two products are added together. The addition and the sum should be written on the recording sheet.

5. Player 2 repeats the same steps.

6. The two players compare their sums. The player with the sum closest to 100 without going over is the winner for the round. That player circles the sum on the recording sheet.

7. All the Digit Cards are gathered, reshuffled, and placed facedown on the table. Round 2 begins and continues in the same way.

8. After 5 rounds, the player with the most circled sums is the winner.

Multiply to Make 100			
	Digit Cards Chosen	**Multiplication Facts**	**Addition**
Example:	8, 7, 3, 9	9 x 8 = 72	72
		3 x 7 = 21	+ 21
			93
Round 1			

Place the decimals in order on the number line.
Use only those decimals with a 3 or greater in the tenths place.

29

1.

```
←——+————————————+————————————+——→
   16           16.50         17
```

16.65   16.55   16.95   16.35   16.25   16.85   16.45   16.15

Use figures 1–4 to answer questions 2–4.

350–351

1   2   3   4

2. Which figure has the smallest area? _____

3. Which figure has the greatest area? _____

4. What two figures have the same area? _____

Solve the problems.

386

5. Barb is driving 285 miles to visit
   her sister. She has 112 miles to go.
   How many miles has Barb already driven? _____

6. Pam is baking brownies. She has 20 ounces
   of sugar. The recipe calls for two pounds of
   sugar. How much more sugar does Pam need? _____

DRAW

WRITE

12 x 12 Cover-Up

X	1	2	3	4	5	6	7	8	9	10	11	12
1												
2												
3												
4												
5												
6												
7												
8												
9												
10												
11												
12												

12 x 12 Multiplication Table and Counters

12 x 12 Cover-Up

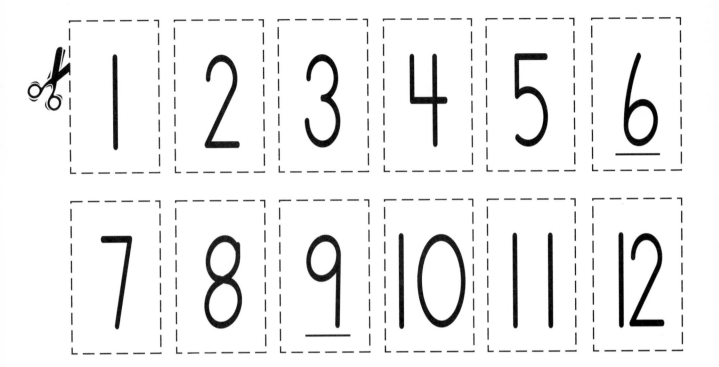

1–12 Factor Cards

Grade 4

Odds Are Even

◆ MATERIALS

Odds Are Even Game Board cardstock, one 1–6 number cube, paper, pencil, game markers

◆ DIRECTIONS

1. Make a tally box like the one below to record the outcome of each game.

2. Players decide who will be "Odd" and "Even" and place their markers on the START circle. The "Even" player uses the EVEN track. The "Odd" player uses the ODD track. Before beginning to play, each player makes a prediction about which player will win the game.

3. Players alternate turns rolling the number cube. If the number is odd, the "Odd" player moves his or her marker one space toward the WIN box. The "Even" player moves her or his marker one space toward the WIN box if the number is even.

4. The first player to reach the WIN box is the winner. Players make a tally to record whether the "Even" or "Odd" player was the winner.

5. Players should play several games as quickly as possible and record the winner of each one. For each game, players compare the result with their predictions.

Even	Odd

25 Write the correct words for the following numbers.
Solve only those problems with a 3 or greater in the tenths place.

1. 17.47 _____

2. 17.71 _____

3. 17.10 _____

4. 17.77 _____

5. 17.57 _____

30 Write the decimal and fraction names for each model.

6.

_____

7.
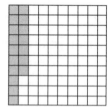
_____

23 Write the value of the 7 in each number.

8. 46.75 _____   **9.** 63.87 _____

10. 71.90 _____   **11.** 17.22 _____

12. 18.07 _____   **13.** 701.25 _____

DRAW

WRITE

_____
_____
_____
_____
_____
_____
_____
_____

PRACTICE

Today's Number: 18

Name _____

Add the decimals. Solve only problems with a 3 or greater in the tenths place.

1. 18.99
   + 19.41

2. 18.01
   + 16.22

3. 28.45
   + 45.32

4. 76.33
   + 33.56

Read each question and circle the best answer.

5. What is the best estimate of the weight of a book, 1 ounce or 1 pound?

6. What is the best estimate of the length of your foot, 9 inches or 9 feet?

7. What is the best estimate of the length of your classroom, 20 centimeters or 20 meters?

Use the picture to answer questions 8–10.

8. If you draw 3 shapes out of the jar without looking, which of these combinations is a possible outcome?

9. Which shape is most likely to be drawn? _____

10. Why do you think so? _____

DRAW

WRITE

_____

_____

_____

_____

_____

_____

_____

_____

1 2 3 4 5

6 7 8 9

1 2 3 4 5

6 7 8 9

Find the Product

◆ MATERIALS

2 sets of 0–9 Digit Cards cardstock (20 cards), paper, pencil

◆ DIRECTIONS

1. Remove both zeroes from the Digit Cards and set them aside.

2. Each player makes a recording sheet like the one shown below.

3. Each player shuffles a set of Digit Cards. The cards are placed facedown on the table.

4. Both players turn over the top card in their stacks at the same time and place them faceup on the table.

5. Both players work independently to determine the product of the two numbers and write the multiplication fact family for that set of numbers. The first player to correctly write the product and the fact family wins the round and takes both cards.

6. If a player thinks an error has been made, he or she can challenge the winner. If an error has been made, the player who made the challenge takes both cards.

7. Play continues until all the cards have been used. The player with more cards is the winner.

	Factor	Factor	Product	Fact Family
Example:	8	7	56	$8 \times 7 = 56$ $7 \times 8 = 56$
				$56 \div 7 = 8$ $56 \div 8 = 7$
1.				
2.				
3.				

Today's Number:

19

Name _____

23, 27 **Compare the decimals using <, >, or =. Solve only those problems with a 3 or greater in the tenths place.**

1. 19.59 ____ 19.90

2. 19.90 ____ 19.9

3. 90.19 ____ 9.19

4. 99.93 ____ 99.39

270–271 **Use the graph to answer questions 5–8.**

5. How many students like strawberry ice cream best? _____

6. What ice cream flavor is the favorite of most students? _____

7. How many more students like vanilla than rocky road? _____

8. What is the least favorite ice cream flavor of the students surveyed? _____

Favorite Ice Cream Flavor	
Vanilla	🍦🍦
Chocolate	🍦🍦🍦🍦🍦
Strawberry	🍦🍦🍦
Rocky Road	🍦🍦

🍦 = 4

396–397 **Use the table to solve the problem.**

9. Jenna, Lisa, Jody, and Diane went out to dinner. Each girl chose a different item from the menu. Jenna did not eat pizza. Diane did not eat egg rolls. Lisa wanted extra lettuce on her tacos. Jody ordered cheese on her hamburger. What did each friend have for dinner?

	Jenna	Lisa	Jody	Diane
pizza				
tacos				
hamburger				
egg rolls				

DRAW

WRITE

_____
_____
_____
_____
_____
_____
_____

Answer each question.

102, 387

1. Write 3 ways to make 200.

_____

_____

_____

2. Write 3 ways to make 100.

_____

_____

_____

Draw each quadrilateral. Then write a brief description of each one.

312–313

3. rhombus

_____

_____

4. rectangle

_____

_____

5. trapezoid

6. square

_____

_____

_____

_____

DRAW

WRITE

_____

_____

_____

_____

_____

_____

_____

_____

Weekly Newsletter

Each week your child will be bringing home Make & Take activities that have been made and used in class. These activities will provide you with materials to help your child explore mathematical concepts. For additional hints, definitions, or explanations refer to the *Math to Know* handbook pages listed below each activity title.

Playing **12 x 12 Cover-Up** will help your child remember basic multiplication facts.

12 X 12 COVER-UP

Multiplication Fact Strategies: 66–73

1. The object is to be the first player to get 4 counters in one row or column on the Multiplication Table.

2. Each player uses 15 counters that are the same color.

3. Put the shaded Factor Cards into one bag and the unshaded cards into the other bag.

4. Players take turns drawing a card from each bag and finding the product of the numbers.

5. Players decide where to place their counters on the Multiplication Table. The Factor Cards are placed back into the correct bags.

6. For each counter placed, the player must state the complete multiplication sentence.

7. The first player to get 4 counters in one row or column is the winner.

In school, we have also been learning about dividing by 1-digit numbers. You will help your child remember what we have learned by playing **Divide to Make 5**.

DIVIDE TO MAKE 5

Division Facts and Concepts: 74–85
Dividing by a 1-Digit Number: 184–185

1. The object of the game is to have the quotient closest to 5 without going over.

2. Each player makes a recording sheet like the one below. The Digit Cards are shuffled and placed facedown on the table.

3. Player 1 draws 4 cards and arranges 3 of the cards into a two-digit by one-digit division problem that will yield the quotient closest to 5. The remaining Digit Card is set aside.

4. Player 1 records the chosen Digit Cards on the recording sheet. Then that player writes and solves the division problem. Player 2 repeats the same steps.

5. The players compare their quotients. The player with the quotient closer to 5 without going over is the winner for the round and circles the quotient on the recording sheet. If both players have the same quotient but different remainders, the player with the smaller remainder wins the round and only the remainder is circled on the recording sheet.

6. All the cards are gathered, reshuffled, and placed facedown on the table. Round 2 begins and continues in the same way.

7. After 5 rounds, the player with the most circled quotients or remainders is the winner.

Divide to Make 5

	Digit Cards Chosen	Division Fact	Solution
Example:	3, 8, 9		4 R2
		9)38	9)38
Round 1			

Today's Number: **21**

Name _____

Write the fraction for the shaded part of each picture.

212–213

1.

_____

2.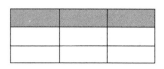

_____

3.

_____

4.

_____

5.

_____

6.

_____

Write each number in standard form.

5–9

7. twenty-one _____

8. two hundred twenty-seven _____

9. six thousand, forty-five _____

10. forty thousand, one hundred ten _____

Solve each problem.

350–351
348–349

11. Karin's room is 16 feet wide and 8 feet long. What is the area of

Karin's room?_____ What is the perimeter? _____

136–137

12. Kristen reads 113 pages in her book every night. What is
the best estimate of the number of pages she reads in 1 week? _____

DRAW

WRITE

250 or Bust!

0 1 2 3 4

5 6 7 8 9

0 1 2 3 4

5 6 7 8 9

0–9 Digit Cards

Grade 4

Measurement Match-Up

◆ MATERIALS

1 set of Measurement Cards I cardstock (15 cards) and 1 set of Measurement Cards II cardstock (15 cards)

◆ DIRECTIONS

1. Shuffle the cards and place them facedown on the table in a 5×6 array.

2. Players take turns turning over two cards, reading them, and comparing them.

3. If the cards are of equal value, the player who turned them over keeps both cards. If the cards do not match, they are turned facedown again. Play passes to the other player.

4. When all the cards have been matched, the player with the most cards is the winner.

There are 1000 milliliters in 1 liter, so these cards match.

212–213

Draw a picture to show each fraction.
Draw pictures only for fractions less than one whole.

1. $\frac{5}{6}$

2. $\frac{3}{10}$

3. $\frac{7}{14}$

4. $\frac{2}{3}$

5. $\frac{6}{6}$

6. $\frac{1}{2}$

314–315

Tell whether each triangle is equilateral, isosceles, or scalene.

7.

8.

9.

_____   _____   _____

82–85

Solve each problem.

10. $50 \div 5 =$ _____

11. $21 \div 7 =$ _____

12. $108 \div 12 =$ _____

13. $72 \div 9 =$ _____

14. $56 \div 8 =$ _____

15. $54 \div 9 =$ _____

DRAW

WRITE

_____
_____
_____
_____
_____
_____
_____
_____
_____

PRACTICE

Today's Number: 23

Name _____

Add the fractions. Draw a picture to help you.
Solve only those problems with answers that are less than one whole.

1. $\frac{3}{5} + \frac{1}{5} =$ _____

2. $\frac{4}{8} + \frac{2}{8} =$ _____

3. $\frac{6}{9} + \frac{3}{9} =$ _____

4. $\frac{7}{12} + \frac{4}{12} =$ _____

5. $\frac{5}{10} + \frac{3}{10} =$ _____

6. $\frac{2}{7} + \frac{1}{7} =$ _____

Find each sum or difference.

7. 83,678
   + 52,091

8. 72,062
   − 34,199

9. 56,482
   + 28,679

Write the name of each polygon.

10.

_____

11.

_____

12.

_____

13.

_____

DRAW

WRITE

_____
_____
_____
_____
_____
_____
_____
_____

Fraction Word Find

Name_____

FRACTION RULE	WORD LIST
Example: $\frac{2}{3}$ of the letters in the word are *m*.	*Example:* mom
1. $\frac{3}{7}$ of the letters in the word are vowels.	
2. $\frac{3}{4}$ of the letters in the word are tall consonants.	
3. $\frac{1}{4}$ of the letters in the word are the same.	
4. $\frac{2}{3}$ of the letters in the word are consonants.	
5. $\frac{1}{5}$ of the letters in the word are vowels.	
6. My Own Rule:	
SCORE:	

Fraction/Decimal Comparing

♦ MATERIALS

1 set of Fraction/Decimal Cards I cardstock (20 cards) and 1 set of Fraction/Decimal Cards II cardstock (20 cards)

♦ DIRECTIONS

1. Shuffle the cards. The cards then are dealt into two facedown stacks, one for each player.

2. Both players turn over the top card in their stacks. Each player reads the decimal or fraction on the card aloud.

3. Players then compare the two cards. The player with the higher card keeps both cards. If the two cards are equal, consider it a tie. Each player keeps his or her card and two new cards are turned over.

4. Play continues until all the cards have been turned over and compared.

5. The winner is the player with the most cards.

$\frac{8}{10}$ or 80 hundredths, is greater than 75 hundredths. I get to keep both cards.

232 Subtract the fractions. Solve only those problems with answers that are less than one whole.

1. $\frac{4}{5} - \frac{1}{5} =$ _____

2. $\frac{5}{7} - \frac{2}{7} =$ _____

3. $\frac{8}{12} - \frac{6}{12} =$ _____

4. $\frac{8}{9} - \frac{1}{9} =$ _____

5. $\frac{12}{10} - \frac{2}{10} =$ _____

6. $\frac{3}{6} - \frac{2}{6} =$ _____

318–319 Tell whether each picture shows a reflection (flip), translation (slide), or rotation (turn).

7.

8.

9.

_____ _____ _____

392–393 Solve each problem.

10. Ken, Janet, and Sandra played a computer game. Ken scored 412 points and Janet scored 318 points. If the three players scored a total of 920 points, how many points did Sandra score? _____

11. A box can hold 9 yo-yos. How many boxes are needed to hold 29 yo-yos? _____

    How did you solve the problem? _____

DRAW

WRITE

_____
_____
_____
_____
_____
_____
_____
_____
_____

Write a fraction and a decimal for each picture. Solve only those problems with answers that are less than one whole.

1.  _____

2. 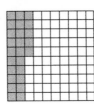 _____

3. 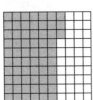 _____

4. 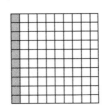 _____

338–339

Write the time that is $1\frac{1}{2}$ hours later than the time shown on each clock.

5.  _____

6. _____

7.  _____

174–175

Write each product.

8. 27
  × 8

9. 49
  × 7

10. 31
  × 9

11. 56
  × 4

DRAW

WRITE

_____
_____
_____
_____
_____
_____
_____
_____

Weekly Newsletter

Each week your child will be bringing home Make & Take activities that have been made and used in class. These activities will provide you with materials to help your child explore mathematical concepts. For additional hints, definitions, or explanations refer to the *Math to Know* handbook pages listed below each activity title.

250 or Bust! is a game that will allow your child to practice multiplying and problem solving.

250 OR BUST!

Estimating Products: 136–137
Multiplying a 2-Digit Number: 174–175

1. The object of the game is to be the player with the product closest to 250 without going over.

2. Each player uses one set of 0–9 Digit Cards. Each player shuffles her or his cards and places them facedown on the table.

3. Player 1 turns over the top 4 cards in his or her stack. That player arranges 3 of the cards into a 2-digit by 1-digit multiplication problem that will yield a product close to 250 without going over. The player discards the card that seems least helpful.

4. Player 1 records the Digit Cards chosen and the multiplication problem on the recording sheet. Then that player solves the problem.

5. Player 2 repeats the steps outlined above.

6. Players compare their products. The player with the product closest to 250 without going over is the winner of the round. That player circles the product on her or his recording sheet.

7. After 5 rounds, the player with more circled products is the winner.

250 or Bust

	Digit Cards Chosen	Multiplication Problem	Solution
Example:	3, 5, 7	35 × 7	35 × 7 245
Round 1			

This week we have been studying fractions. Your child has been learning that a fraction represents a part of a set. **Fraction Word Find** uses fractions in an interesting way.

FRACTION WORD FIND

Fraction Concepts: 210–211
Fraction of a Group: 214–215

1. Start by making a copy of the fraction rule list on the Recording Sheet your child has brought home. This gives you the rules for the words you will be looking for.

2. The object is to find or think of as many words as possible within a limited amount of time for each fraction rule. Using books, magazines, or newspapers for help is allowed.

3. Set a time limit, such as fifteen minutes, for the activity. Within that time limit, players try to find or think of as many words as they can to fit each fraction rule.

4. When time is up, both you and your child create your own fraction rule. Write these rules down and allow yourselves five more minutes to find words that fit your rules.

5. When the activity has been completed, exchange word lists with your child. Check each other's words to be sure they fit the fraction rules. Score 1 point for each correct word. The player with the highest score is the winner.

Use doubles and doubles + 1 to find each answer.

42–43

1. 12 + 12 = _____   12 + 13 = _____

2. 15 + 15 = _____   15 + 16 = _____

3. 20 + 20 = _____   20 + 21 = _____

4. 25 + 25 = _____   25 + 26 = _____

5. 50 + 50 = _____   50 + 51 = _____

Use the coordinate grid to answer questions 6–13. Name the ordered pair for each point.

258–259

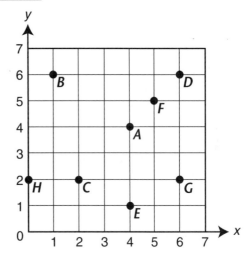

6. F _____   **7.** H _____

8. A _____   **9.** D _____

10. E _____   **11.** B _____

12. G _____   **13.** C _____

Write each quotient.

82–85

14. 72 ÷ 9 = _____   **15.** 56 ÷ 7 = _____   **16.** 64 ÷ 8 = _____

17. What pattern do you see? _____

DRAW

WRITE

_____
_____
_____
_____
_____
_____
_____
_____

Find the Shapes

Name_____

Shape	Sketch	Items at School	Items at Home
Sphere			
Cylinder			
Cone			
Square			
Pyramid			
Cube			
Rectangular Prism			
Triangular Prism			

There's Just One Difference

◆ MATERIALS

1 set of Attribute Cards cardstock (24 cards)

◆ DIRECTIONS

1. Shuffle the Attribute Cards and, keeping them facedown, deal 12 cards to each player.

2. Players look at their cards but do not show them to each other.

3. Player 1 starts the game by selecting one card to place faceup on the table.

4. Player 2 selects a card that differs from Player 1's card in only one way and places it beside the first card. For example, if Player 1 begins with a large red circle, Player 2 can follow it with a large red square or triangle (only the shape is different), a large circle that is not red (only the color is different), or a small red circle (only the size is different).

5. Play alternates back and forth with each player adding to the lineup in the same way.

6. A player who does not have a card to play that differs from the last card in just one way loses the game. Otherwise, the player who uses all of her or his cards first is the winner.

I can follow a small green triangle with a small green square.

180–181 **Write each product.**

1. 27 × 15 = _____   2. 27 × 16 = _____   3. 27 × 17 = _____

4. 27 × 18 = _____   5. 27 × 19 = _____   6. 27 × 20 = _____

7. What pattern do you see in the products? _____

_____

308–309 **Tell what type of angle the clock hands form.**
Then write the time shown on each clock.

8.

angle: _____

time: _____

9.

angle: _____

time: _____

10.

angle: _____

time: _____

82–83 **Write a multiplication fact family for each set of numbers.**

11. 3, 9, 27   12. 7, 8, 56

_____ _____   _____ _____

_____ _____   _____ _____

DRAW

WRITE

_____

_____

_____

_____

_____

_____

_____

_____

146–152
159–167

Write each sum or difference.

1. 208 − 176 = _____

2. 208 + 112 = _____

3. 2080 − 1760 = _____

4. 2080 + 1120 = _____

206–207

Tell whether each number is divisible by 2, 5, 10, 3, and 9.

	÷ by 2?	÷ by 5?	÷ by 10?	÷ by 3?	÷ by 9?
5. 45	_____	_____	_____	_____	_____
6. 63	_____	_____	_____	_____	_____
7. 72	_____	_____	_____	_____	_____

268

Use the schedule to answer questions 8–11.

Earth Day Events

EVENT	STARTING TIME	ENDING TIME
Recycling Show	10:00	11:00
Sidewalk Art	10:00	12:00
Save the Earth Puppet Show	11:45	12:15
Community Clean Up	12:00	3:30
Parade	3:30	5:00
Dinner	5:00	7:00

8. If you go to the Recycling Show, can you still see the Sidewalk Art? _____

9. How much longer is the Dinner than the Parade? _____

10. Which lasts longer, Community Clean Up or Dinner? _____

11. How many hours are there from the beginning of the events until the end? _____

DRAW

WRITE

1 2 3 4 5

6 1 2 3 4

5 6 4 5 6

7 8 9

Write each number in standard form.

5–10

1. forty thousand, twenty-nine _____

2. two hundred twelve thousand, eight hundred fifteen _____

Write the value of each underlined digit.

348

3. 6<u>8</u>3,294 _____   4. <u>4</u>51,870 _____

Write the perimeter of each polygon.

396–397

5.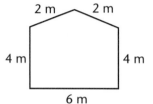

6.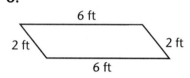

7.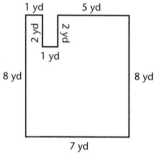

_____   _____   _____

Solve each problem.

8. Ed, Joe, Sue, and Kim ran in a race. Sue finished ahead of Ed, but behind Kim. Joe finished behind Sue, but ahead of Ed. Who won the race? _____

9. Luke is taller than Joan, but shorter than Sam. Pat is shorter than Sam, but taller than Luke. Bob is taller than Sam.

   Who is the shortest? _____   Who is the tallest? _____

DRAW

WRITE

_____

_____

_____

_____

_____

_____

_____

136–137 Write an estimate for each product.

1. $28 \times 4 =$ _____

2. $36 \times 5 =$ _____

3. $11 \times 6 =$ _____

4. $352 \times 8 =$ _____

5. $95 \times 5 =$ _____

6. $478 \times 4 =$ _____

212–213 Write a fraction for each shaded part.

7.

8.

9.

____   ____   ____

30 Write a fraction and decimal for each shaded part.

10.

_____

11.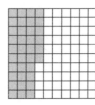

_____

12.

_____

13.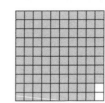

_____

DRAW

WRITE

_____

_____

_____

_____

_____

_____

_____

Weekly Newsletter

Each week your child will be bringing home Make & Take activities that have been made and used in class. These activities will provide you with materials to help your child explore mathematical concepts. For additional hints, definitions, or explanations refer to the *Math to Know* handbook pages listed below each activity title.

Find the Shapes is a scavenger hunt activity. You and your child can search for common items around the house that are in the shape of various three-dimensional figures.

FIND THE SHAPES

Names for Solid Figures: 328–329
Drawing Solid Figures: 426–427

1. Make your own copy of the Recording Sheet your child has brought home. You can make sketches of the shapes on the list. Your child will learn by watching you draw. This is a great time to discuss how difficult it is to draw three-dimensional shapes in two dimensions!

2. You and your child should take your Recording Sheets and walk around the inside and outside of your home, looking for objects that are in the shape of the ones on the list. Put a time limit on how long you can search, and be sure you work independently of each other. Find as many objects as you can for each shape. Record each object you find in the correct box on the Recording Sheet. There may be shapes that you will not find.

3. When the time is up, you and your child can share what you found. Did you both find some of the same objects? Were there any shapes neither of you found? Are all the shapes recorded in the correct places on the Recording Sheet?

4. A trip to the grocery store with your child can turn into the discovery of many interesting geometric shapes. Packages come in a wide variety of shapes, and it can be fun finding them.

Division Race can be a fun way for your child to continue math practice at home.

DIVISION RACE

Dividing by 1 Digit: 184–185
Checking Division: 205

1. Both you and your child will need to make a recording sheet like the one shown below. Put all the Division Race Cards in the paper bag and shake it up.

2. Player 1 reaches into the bag and draws 3 cards. He or she creates a two-digit by one-digit division problem with the numbers drawn.

3. Both players record the division problem on their recording sheets. Then the players race to solve the problem. Both players must check the solution using multiplication. The first player to correctly solve the division problem and check it wins the round and circles the quotient on his or her recording sheet.

4. Round 2 begins with Player 2 reaching into the bag, drawing 3 cards, and creating the division problem for the round. Players race to solve and check the problem.

5. After repeating these steps for 5 rounds, the player with the most circled quotients is the winner of the game.

Division Race

	Numbers Drawn	Division Problem	Multiplication Check
Example:	3, 6, 8	6 R2	
		6)38	6 × 6 = 36 + 2 = 38
		−36	
Round 1		2	

Weekly Newsletter

Each week your child will be bringing home Make & Take activities that have been made and used in class. These activities will provide you with materials to help your child explore mathematical concepts. For additional hints, definitions, or explanations refer to the *Math to Know* handbook pages listed below each activity title.

Your child has been exploring geometric ideas, such as congruence and symmetry. We used an activity called **Exploring Shapes**. You can reinforce these ideas by helping your child find things around the house that are congruent or that have lines of symmetry. Observe your child to see if he or she has a basic understanding of these geometric ideas.

EXPLORING SHAPES

Congruent Figures: 317
Symmetry: 322–323
Naming Polygons: 311
Names for Solid Figures: 328–329

1. Have your child use the Shape Pieces to show you pieces that are congruent and pieces that are not congruent.

2. Have your child describe any lines of symmetry for the different pieces.

3. Your child can use all seven pieces to make one large square.

4. Your child should go on a scavenger hunt, looking for items that are circles, squares, pentagons, hexagons, and octagons. She or he should make a list showing which shapes were the easiest and most difficult to find.

5. Next, your child should look for items that are shaped like cones, cylinders, pyramids, and spheres. Again, she or he should make a list showing which shapes were the easiest and most difficult to find.

Another activity this week was the **Fraction Kit** game. Your child is developing the idea of equivalent fractions with the use of visual models.

FRACTION KIT

Fraction Concepts: 212–226
Adding Fractions: 227–229

1. All the fraction pieces are placed faceup on the table. The white fraction labels are put back in the paper bag.

2. Each player starts with the "1 Whole" strip faceup in front of him or her. The object is to be the first player to cover the "1 Whole" strip exactly with fraction pieces.

3. Players take turns drawing a fraction label from the paper bag and selecting a matching fraction piece from the array on the table. Then the fraction piece is placed on the "1 Whole" strip and the fraction label is put back into the bag. For example, if the fraction label marked "$\frac{1}{3}$" is drawn from the bag, pick up a fraction piece marked "$\frac{1}{3}$" from the table and begin covering the "1 Whole" strip.

4. The first player to exactly cover her or his "1 Whole" strip is the winner.

5. As a variation, try to cover two "Whole" strips by continuing play after your first "1 Whole" strip is completely covered.

Some things to notice:

- Can your child demonstrate equivalent fractions such as $\frac{2}{4}$ and $\frac{1}{2}$?

- Does your child understand how the fractional part relates to the whole?

Take every opportunity to point out fractional parts in items you use every day. Using recipes when cooking is a great way to help your child continue to visualize fractions.

Have fun this week investigating two- and three-dimensional shapes and fractions with your child.

Name _____

NUMBER SENSE

Choose the best answer or write a response for each question.

1. What is the value of the digit 3 in 5.38?

(A) 3 tens

(B) 3 tenths

(C) 3 hundreds

(D) 3 hundredths

2. Which diagram shows $\frac{3}{4}$?

(A) [diagram]

(B) [diagram]

(C) [diagram]

(D) [diagram]

3. Which number shows

34 hundreds 2 tens 6 ones

in standard form?

(A)   326

(B)   3,426

(C)   340,26

(D) 340,026

4. Which decimal and fraction describes the shaded part of the model below?

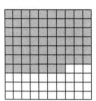

(A) 0.67 and $\frac{67}{100}$

(B) 67 and $\frac{67}{100}$

(C) 0.33 and $\frac{33}{100}$

(D) 33 and $\frac{33}{100}$

5. Which group of numbers is in order from **greatest** to **least**?

(A) 48.00   0.480   4.800   0.048

(B) 48.00   4.800   0.480   0.048

(C) 0.048   0.480   4.800   48.00

(D) 4.800   0.048   48.00   0.480

6. Which number has a 7 in the hundred thousands place?

(A) 3,483,721

(B) 3,687,421

(C) 4,783,621

(D) 6,373,421

Score: Circle the number of correct responses out of 6 items in this section.   1   2   3   4   5   6

BASIC OPERATIONS

7. Subtract.

$$\begin{array}{r} \$403 \\ -\$125 \\ \hline \end{array}$$

(A) $278

(B) $528

(C) $628

(D) $738

8. Add.

$$\begin{array}{r} 69.43 \\ +\,11.90 \\ \hline \end{array}$$

(A) 57.53

(B) 64.13

(C) 70.33

(D) Not Given

9. Multiply.

$$\begin{array}{r} 35 \\ \times 22 \\ \hline \end{array}$$

(A) 140

(B) 216

(C) 700

(D) 770

10. Complete the quotient.

$$66 \div 8 = 8\,\text{R}\,\underline{\hspace{1cm}}$$

(A) 1

(B) 2

(C) 3

(D) 4

11. Which number completes the fact family?

$$6 \times 7 = \underline{\hspace{1cm}} \text{ so } \underline{\hspace{1cm}} \div 6 = 7$$

(A) 10

(B) 13

(C) 21

(D) 42

12. Which pair of numbers rounds to 1,000?

(A) 1,030 and 1,300

(B) 1,519 and 488

(C) 1,489 and 927

(D) 1,398 and 920

Score: Circle the number of correct responses out of 6 items in this section.

   1   2   3   4   5   6

GEOMETRY AND MEASUREMENT

13. Which is the name the polygon?

- (A) hexagon
- (B) pentagon
- (C) quadrilateral
- (D) octagon

14. Ana's room measures 17 feet by 22 feet. What is the perimeter of the room?

- (A) 39 feet
- (B) 70 feet
- (C) 78 feet
- (D) 100 feet

15. What is a reasonable estimate for the deep end of a swimming pool?

- (A) about 6 inches
- (B) about 6 feet
- (C) about 6 yards
- (D) about 6 miles

16. Choose the best unit to measure the weight of a sack of potatoes.

- (A) ounce
- (B) pound
- (C) ton
- (D) inch

17. What time will it be four hours from the time shown on the clock?

- (A) 4:30
- (B) 5:30
- (C) 6:30
- (D) 7:30

18. Jose has 3 quarters, 2 dimes, and 1 nickel. How much money does he have?

- (A) $0.75
- (B) $0.85
- (C) $1.00
- (D) $1.15

Score: Circle the number of correct responses out of 6 items in this section.   1   2   3   4   5   6

PATTERNS AND ALGEBRAIC REASONING

19. Look at the number pattern.

257 357 457 557 657

What is the number after 657?

- (A) 668
- (B) 677
- (C) 757
- (D) 777

20. Complete the sentence.

When you multiply 945 by 1, the product equals _____ .

- (A) 0
- (B) 1
- (C) 945
- (D) 946

21. Which number completes the equation?

_____ × 7 = 63

- (A) 9
- (B) 10
- (C) 11
- (D) 12

22. Complete the equation.

46 ÷ 8 = _____ R _____

- (A) 6 R 5
- (B) 5 R 6
- (C) 4 R 6
- (D) 4 R 5

Use the grid to answer questions 23–24.

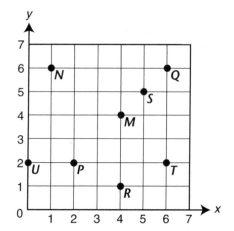

23. Name the ordered pair for Point *R*.

- (A) (6, 6)
- (B) (5, 5)
- (C) (4, 1)
- (D) (1, 4)

24. Name the point on the grid with the ordered pair (4, 4).

- (A) Point *N*
- (B) Point *Q*
- (C) Point *R*
- (D) Point *M*

Score: Circle the number of correct responses out of 6 items in this section.

1   2   3   4   5   6

PROBLEM SOLVING AND DATA ANALYSIS

25. Four cars are parked in a row. Ted's car is behind Martha's. Justin's car is in front of Martha's, but behind Sonia's car. Which two cars are in the middle?

- (A) Sonia and Ted
- (B) Justin and Martha
- (C) Ted and Justin
- (D) Martha and Sonia

26. Use the pictograph.

Favorite Snack	
Fruit	♡♡♡♡♡
Cereal	♡♡♡♡
Popcorn	♡♡♡♡♡♡

KEY: ♡ = 1 student

Which snack has more votes than cereal, but fewer than popcorn?

- (A) Fruit
- (B) Cereal
- (C) Popcorn
- (D) Not Given

27. You reach into a bag with 4 green cubes and 9 black cubes. Which cube are you more likely to pull out? Why do you think so?

Answer: _____

Use the table to answer questions 28–29.

Popular Bulbs Sold

Type	Number Sold
Tulip	956
Hyacinth	515
Daffodil	924
Crocus	932

28. Which bulb is the most popular?

- (A) Crocus
- (B) Daffodil
- (C) Hyacinth
- (D) Tulip

29. Suppose 50 more daffodils are sold. How would the data in the table change?

Answer: _____

_____

30. You pull 2 shapes from the bag without looking. Which combination is *not* a possible outcome?

- (A)
- (B)
- (C)
- (D)

Score: Circle the number of correct responses out of 6 items in this section.   1   2   3   4   5   6

Name _____

PRACTICE 1 • Whole Number Concepts

Directions: Choose the best answer to each question.

SAMPLES

A. Which is a multiple of 7?

- (A) 15
- (B) 28
- (C) 32
- (D) 45

B. What is 763 rounded to the nearest 10?

- (A) 800
- (B) 770
- (C) 760
- (D) 700

C. Which number means $3000 + 60 + 2$?

- (A) 362
- (B) 3062
- (C) 3620
- (D) 30,602

D. Which is an odd number?

- (A) 12
- (B) 23
- (C) 32
- (D) 44

> **Tips and Reminders**
> - Be sure to look at all the answer choices before you choose an answer. Try out each answer choice to find the one that is correct.
> - After choosing an answer, read the question again to make sure you have answered it correctly.

PRACTICE

1. Which number shows two thousand four hundred twenty-one?

- (A) 242
- (B) 2421
- (C) 20,421
- (D) 24,201

2. What is the value of the **9** in 32,794?

- (A) 9000
- (B) 900
- (C) 90
- (D) 9

Go On →

3. Which number is 10 less than 55?

Ⓐ 40

Ⓑ 45

Ⓒ 54

Ⓓ 65

4. Which number comes next?

2, 7, 12, 17, ___?___ . . .

Ⓐ 18

Ⓑ 19

Ⓒ 21

Ⓓ 22

5. Which is an even number?

Ⓐ 23

Ⓑ 36

Ⓒ 47

Ⓓ 51

6. What is 379 rounded to the nearest 100?

Ⓐ 400

Ⓑ 380

Ⓒ 370

Ⓓ 300

7. Which shape comes next in this pattern?

◇ ☆ ○ ○ □ ◇ ☆ ○ ○ __?__

Ⓐ ◇

Ⓑ ☆

Ⓒ ○

Ⓓ □

8. Which is a multiple of 8?

Ⓐ 4

Ⓑ 24

Ⓒ 28

Ⓓ 30

9. What is the value of the **3** in 1370?

Ⓐ 3 ones

Ⓑ 3 tens

Ⓒ 3 hundreds

Ⓓ 3 thousands

10. Which number means 2000 + 10 + 8?

Ⓐ 218

Ⓑ 2018

Ⓒ 2108

Ⓓ 20,108

11. Which is a factor of 30?

Ⓐ 6

Ⓑ 7

Ⓒ 8

Ⓓ 9

12. Which number is between 504 and 540?

Ⓐ 415

Ⓑ 451

Ⓒ 514

Ⓓ 541

Stop

Name _____

PRACTICE 2 • Fractions and Decimals

Directions: Choose the best answer to each question.

SAMPLES

A. Which fraction is equivalent to $\frac{1}{2}$?

Ⓐ $\frac{2}{5}$ Ⓒ $\frac{3}{5}$

Ⓑ $\frac{2}{4}$ Ⓓ $\frac{3}{4}$

B. Which number is less than 2.35?

Ⓐ 5.23

Ⓑ 3.25

Ⓒ 2.5

Ⓓ 2.21

Tips and Reminders

• Look at the pictures carefully. Draw your own pictures if that will help you find the answer.

• To compare fractions, change them to "like" fractions with the same denominator.

PRACTICE

1. Which fraction is shaded?

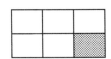

Ⓐ $\frac{1}{3}$ Ⓒ $\frac{1}{5}$

Ⓑ $\frac{1}{4}$ Ⓓ $\frac{1}{6}$

2. Which fraction is greater than $\frac{2}{3}$?

Ⓐ $\frac{3}{4}$ Ⓒ $\frac{1}{2}$

Ⓑ $\frac{2}{5}$ Ⓓ $\frac{2}{6}$

3. Which number sentence is true?

Ⓐ $\frac{1}{2} > \frac{3}{4}$ Ⓒ $\frac{4}{6} = \frac{1}{3}$

Ⓑ $\frac{2}{3} > \frac{1}{2}$ Ⓓ $\frac{3}{4} < \frac{4}{6}$

4. Which fraction is equivalent to $\frac{4}{6}$?

Ⓐ $\frac{3}{7}$ Ⓒ $\frac{2}{3}$

Ⓑ $\frac{4}{5}$ Ⓓ $\frac{1}{4}$

Go On

5. Which list shows the numbers in order from least to greatest?

(A) 2.43, 2.34, 3.23, 3.32

(B) 1.85, 1.78, 1.46, 1.51

(C) 1.05, 1.50, 2.25, 2.55

(D) 2.13, 2.74, 2.47, 2.31

6. Which fraction is greater than $\frac{5}{6}$?

(A) $\frac{1}{2}$ (C) $\frac{4}{6}$

(B) $\frac{3}{4}$ (D) $\frac{11}{12}$

7. Which fraction is shaded?

(A) $\frac{3}{5}$ (C) $\frac{2}{6}$

(B) $\frac{3}{4}$ (D) $\frac{2}{5}$

8. Which number is greatest?

(A) 3.012

(B) 3.021

(C) 3.120

(D) 3.102

9. On a number line, which fraction would be between $\frac{1}{4}$ and $\frac{1}{2}$?

(A) $\frac{1}{5}$ (C) $\frac{2}{8}$

(B) $\frac{1}{3}$ (D) $\frac{3}{6}$

10. Which picture shows $\frac{3}{4}$ shaded?

(A)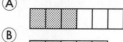

(B)

(C)

(D)

11. Which number sentence is true?

(A) $0.75 = 7.5$

(B) $0.056 = 0.56$

(C) $0.047 = 0.407$

(D) $0.38 = 0.380$

12. Which fraction is less than $\frac{3}{8}$?

(A) $\frac{1}{4}$ (C) $\frac{1}{2}$

(B) $\frac{2}{3}$ (D) $\frac{2}{5}$

13. Which number is least?

(A) 1.325

(B) 1.235

(C) 1.532

(D) 1.352

14. Which picture shows $\frac{2}{3}$ of the boxes shaded?

(A)

(B)

(C)

(D)

Stop

PRACTICE 3 • Number Operations

Directions: Choose the best answer to each question.

SAMPLES

A. Which number goes in the box to complete the number sentence?

$$\square + 3 = 18$$

- (A) 0
- (B) 3
- (C) 15
- (D) 18

B. Which sign goes in the circle?

$$12 \bigcirc 3 = 9$$

$+$ $-$ $\times$ $\div$

(A)   (B)   (C)   (D)

C. What coordinates are shown by the point on the grid?

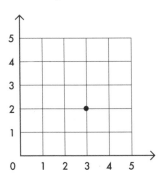

- (A) (3, 2)
- (B) (2, 3)
- (C) (3, 3)
- (D) (4, 3)

Tips and Reminders

- Read each number sentence carefully. Try each answer choice in the number sentence until you find one that is correct.

- In an ordered pair, find the first number by counting to the right. The second number tells how many spaces to count up.

PRACTICE

1. Which number makes this number sentence true?

$$5 \times 4 = 13 + \square$$

4   5   6   7

(A)   (B)   (C)   (D)

2. What is another way to write 4×6?

- (A) $4 + 6$
- (B) $6 \times 6 \times 6 \times 6$
- (C) $6 - 4$
- (D) $6 + 6 + 6 + 6$

Go On →

3. Which sign goes in the circle?

$$44 \bigcirc 0 = 0$$

+   −   ×   ÷

Ⓐ   Ⓑ   Ⓒ   Ⓓ

4.

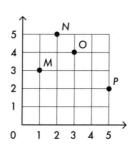

Which point shows the coordinates (2, 5)?

M   N   O   P

Ⓐ   Ⓑ   Ⓒ   Ⓓ

5. Which number makes this number sentence true?

$$28 - 6 = 18 + \square$$

2   3   4   5

Ⓐ   Ⓑ   Ⓒ   Ⓓ

6. What is another way to write 3×9?

Ⓐ $9 \times 9 \times 9$

Ⓑ $9 + 9 + 9$

Ⓒ $3 + 9$

Ⓓ $9 - 3$

7. Which sign goes in the circle?

$$9 \bigcirc 9 = 3 \times 6$$

+   −   ×   ÷

Ⓐ   Ⓑ   Ⓒ   Ⓓ

8. What is another way to write $5 + 5 + 5 + 5 + 5$?

Ⓐ $5 + 5$

Ⓑ $5 \times 5 \times 5 \times 5 \times 5$

Ⓒ 5×5

Ⓓ $5 + 5 \times 5$

9. Which sign goes in the circle?

$$48 \bigcirc 8 = 6$$

+   −   ×   ÷

Ⓐ   Ⓑ   Ⓒ   Ⓓ

10. Which number makes this number sentence true?

$$30 \div 5 = 2 \times \square$$

3   2   1   0

Ⓐ   Ⓑ   Ⓒ   Ⓓ

11.

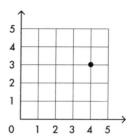

What coordinates are shown by the point on the grid?

Ⓐ (3, 5)   Ⓒ (4, 3)

Ⓑ (3, 4)   Ⓓ (2, 3)

12. Which number sentence is in the same family of facts as $9 - 2 = 7$?

Ⓐ $2 \times 7 = 14$

Ⓑ $2 + 7 = 9$

Ⓒ $2 \times 9 = 18$

Ⓓ $7 - 2 = 5$

Stop

PRACTICE 4 • Geometry

Directions: Choose the best answer to each question.

SAMPLES

A. Which figure is shaped like a sphere?

Ⓐ   Ⓒ

Ⓑ   Ⓓ

B. What is the perimeter of this figure?

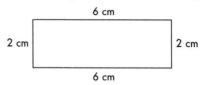

Ⓐ 8 cm

Ⓑ 12 cm

Ⓒ 16 cm

Ⓓ 24 cm

Tips and Reminders

• Use the pictures to find the information you need.

• After choosing an answer, read the question again to make sure you have answered it correctly.

PRACTICE

1. What is the area of this figure in square units?

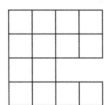

Ⓐ 12

Ⓑ 14

Ⓒ 15

Ⓓ 16

2. Which figure is shaped like a cylinder?

Ⓐ   Ⓒ

Ⓑ   Ⓓ

Go On

3. What is the perimeter of this figure?

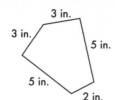

3 in.
3 in.
5 in.
5 in.
2 in.

Ⓐ 6 in.

Ⓑ 11 in.

Ⓒ 15 in.

Ⓓ 18 in.

4. Which figure shows a line of symmetry?

Ⓐ

Ⓒ

Ⓑ

Ⓓ

5. Which line is parallel to $\overleftrightarrow{AB}$?

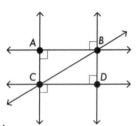

Ⓐ $\overleftrightarrow{CD}$

Ⓑ $\overleftrightarrow{AC}$

Ⓒ $\overleftrightarrow{BD}$

Ⓓ $\overleftrightarrow{CB}$

6. In which pair are the figures congruent?

Ⓐ

Ⓒ

Ⓑ

Ⓓ

7. Which figure below is a pyramid?

Ⓐ

Ⓒ

Ⓑ

Ⓓ

8. Which figure has a line of symmetry?

Ⓐ

Ⓒ

Ⓑ

Ⓓ

Go On

Summer Success: Math

9. What is the area of this rectangle in square units?

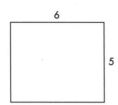

Ⓐ 30

Ⓑ 22

Ⓒ 11

Ⓓ 1

Use the figure below to answer questions 10–11.

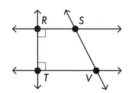

10. Which line is parallel to $\overleftrightarrow{RS}$?

Ⓐ $\overleftrightarrow{RT}$

Ⓑ $\overleftrightarrow{TV}$

Ⓒ $\overleftrightarrow{SV}$

Ⓓ $\overleftrightarrow{TR}$

11. $\overleftrightarrow{SV}$ and $\overleftrightarrow{TV}$ are –

Ⓐ intersecting lines

Ⓑ right angles

Ⓒ parallel lines

Ⓓ congruent figures

12. What is the perimeter of this figure?

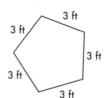

Ⓐ 12 ft

Ⓑ 14 ft

Ⓒ 15 ft

Ⓓ 18 ft

13. Which figure below is a rectangular prism?

14. What is the area of this rectangle in square units?

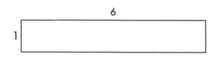

Ⓐ 14

Ⓑ 7

Ⓒ 5

Ⓓ 6

Stop

PRACTICE 5 • Measurement

Directions: Choose the best answer to each question.

SAMPLES

A. Jordan arrived at the bus stop at 7:55. The bus came at 8:15. How many minutes did Jordan wait?

   Ⓐ 15 minutes   Ⓒ 40 minutes

   Ⓑ 20 minutes   Ⓓ 55 minutes

B. Which unit should you use to measure the distance across the United States?

   Ⓐ centimeters   Ⓒ millimeters

   Ⓑ meters   Ⓓ kilometers

Tips and Reminders

- Use the pictures to find the information you need.

- Make an estimate. Check to see if any of the answer choices is close to your estimate.

- Try each answer choice given. Rule out those that make no sense at all.

PRACTICE

1. What temperature is shown on the thermometer?

   Ⓐ 43°F   Ⓒ 34°F

   Ⓑ 36°F   Ⓓ 32°F

2. What time is shown on the clock?

   Ⓐ 1:50   Ⓒ 10:05

   Ⓑ 2:10   Ⓓ 10:12

Go On ➡

3. Dom begins his newspaper route at 5:35. Which clock shows this exact time?

Ⓐ

Ⓑ

Ⓒ

Ⓓ

4. Sarah is looking for a box to ship her skateboard. <u>About</u> how long should the box be?

Ⓐ 3 in.   Ⓒ 10 in.

Ⓑ 3 ft   Ⓓ 10 ft

5. How much money is shown?

Ⓐ $1.25

Ⓑ $1.35

Ⓒ $1.39

Ⓓ $1.75

6. Which unit should you use to measure the length of a soccer field?

Ⓐ yards

Ⓑ inches

Ⓒ tons

Ⓓ miles

7. What temperature is shown on the thermometer?

Ⓐ 102°F   Ⓒ 98°F

Ⓑ 100°F   Ⓓ 96°F

8. One inch equals one mile on the map below. <u>About</u> how far is the bank from the school?

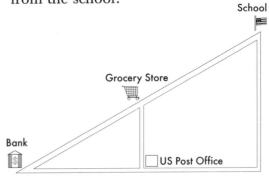

Ⓐ 2 miles

Ⓑ 3 miles

Ⓒ 4 miles

Ⓓ 5 miles

9. Which unit should you use to measure the weight of a hummingbird?

(A) grams

(B) kilograms

(C) gallons

(D) cups

10. Crissy paid 83 cents for an apple and a peach. Which of the following shows exactly how much she paid?

(A)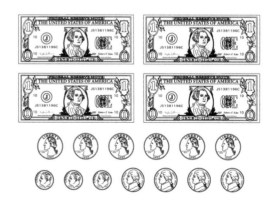

(B)

(C)

(D)

11. Doris began sending e-mail messages at 4:40. Which clock shows this time exactly?

(A)

(B)

(C)

(D)

12. How long is the paper clip chain?

(A) 3 in.

(B) 4 in.

(C) 5 in.

(D) 6 in.

13. Tyree lives on the second floor of an apartment building. <u>About</u> how high from the ground is his window?

(A) 2 feet

(B) 2 yards

(C) 20 feet

(D) 200 yards

14. Below is the amount of money Jenna earned raking leaves. How much did she earn?

(A) $4.40

(B) $5.00

(C) $5.84

(D) $6.00

Stop

PRACTICE 6 • Computation

Directions: Find the answer to each problem. If the correct answer is not given, fill in the bubble for N, "Not Given."

SAMPLES

A. $29 \times 31 =$
- Ⓐ 116
- Ⓑ 879
- Ⓒ 899
- Ⓓ N

B. $248 \div 8 =$
- Ⓐ 31
- Ⓑ 31 R4
- Ⓒ 36
- Ⓓ N

C. $\frac{3}{8} + \frac{1}{8} =$
- Ⓐ $\frac{4}{16}$
- Ⓑ $\frac{2}{8}$
- Ⓒ $\frac{1}{2}$
- Ⓓ N

D. $4.7 + 2.3 =$
- Ⓐ 6.0
- Ⓑ 4.9
- Ⓒ 2.4
- Ⓓ N

Tips and Reminders

- Look at the sign to see if you need to add (+), subtract (−), multiply (×), or divide (÷ or $\overline{)}\ \ $).

- Always check your answer.

- When you add or subtract fractions, be sure to simplify your answer. For example, in sample C, $\frac{3}{8} + \frac{1}{8} = \frac{4}{8}$; $\frac{4}{8}$ can be simplified to $\frac{1}{2}$, which is the correct answer.

- When using numbers with decimals, make sure you line up the decimal points before you add or subtract.

PRACTICE

1.
$$\begin{array}{r} 81 \\ \times\ 17 \end{array}$$
- Ⓐ 1377
- Ⓑ 1387
- Ⓒ 8667
- Ⓓ N

2. $16\overline{)236}$
- Ⓐ 13 R12
- Ⓑ 14
- Ⓒ 14 R12
- Ⓓ N

Go On →

3. 356
  + 24

(A) 332
(B) 370
(C) 390
(D) N

4. $421 - 87 =$

(A) 334
(B) 344
(C) 346
(D) N

5. $2.85
  + 1.15

(A) $1.70
(B) $3.90
(C) $4.00
(D) N

6. $45 + 317 =$

(A) 362
(B) 371
(C) 372
(D) N

7. 32
  × 11

(A) 312
(B) 352
(C) 362
(D) N

8. $516 \div 12 =$

(A) 42
(B) 42 R6
(C) 43
(D) N

9. $\frac{4}{9} + \frac{1}{9} =$

(A) $\frac{5}{9}$
(B) $\frac{4}{9}$
(C) $\frac{3}{9}$
(D) N

10. $26 \times 47 =$

(A) 1122
(B) 1222
(C) 1223
(D) N

11. $\frac{3}{4} - \frac{1}{4} =$

(A) $\frac{3}{16}$
(B) $\frac{1}{4}$
(C) 1
(D) N

12. 406
  − 219

(A) 197
(B) 287
(C) 297
(D) N

13. $9 \times 32 =$

(A) 278
(B) 286
(C) 288
(D) N

14. 23
  17
  + 39

(A) 79
(B) 76
(C) 69
(D) N

Go On

15. 9.6
       + 5.5

    (A) 4.1
    (B) 14.1
    (C) 15.1
    (D) N

16. $8.22 – $3.25 =

    (A) $11.47
    (B) $5.07
    (C) $4.97
    (D) N

17. $736 \div 16 =$

    (A) 45
    (B) 46
    (C) 46 R2
    (D) N

18. $\frac{4}{7} + \frac{3}{7} =$

    (A) 1
    (B) $\frac{1}{7}$
    (C) $\frac{7}{14}$
    (D) N

19. 57
       × 13

    (A) 711
    (B) 721
    (C) 731
    (D) N

20. 318
       – 157

    (A) 61
    (B) 251
    (C) 261
    (D) N

21. $7.89
       – 2.76

    (A) $10.65
    (B) $9.23
    (C) $5.13
    (D) N

22. $8 \times 46 =$

    (A) 368
    (B) 348
    (C) 328
    (D) N

23. $670 \div 15$

    (A) 44
    (B) 44 R10
    (C) 45
    (D) N

24. $\frac{7}{8} - \frac{5}{8} =$

    (A) $\frac{3}{4}$
    (B) $\frac{3}{8}$
    (C) $\frac{1}{4}$
    (D) N

25. $0.99 + 0.20 =$

    (A) 0.79
    (B) 1.09
    (C) 2.99
    (D) N

Stop

Name _____

PRACTICE 7 • Estimation

Directions: Choose the best answer to each question.

SAMPLES

A. The closest estimate of 38 + 11 is –

Ⓐ 30
Ⓑ 40
Ⓒ 50
Ⓓ 60

B. 18 × 12 is between –

Ⓐ 150 and 200
Ⓑ 200 and 250
Ⓒ 250 and 300
Ⓓ 300 and 350

Tips and Reminders
• To estimate, round each number to the nearest ten, hundred, or thousand.

• Use number sense to check your answer.

PRACTICE

1. The closest estimate of 51 + 28 is –

Ⓐ 70
Ⓑ 80
Ⓒ 90
Ⓓ 100

2. The closest estimate of 362 − 184 is –

Ⓐ 18
Ⓑ 20
Ⓒ 180
Ⓓ 200

3. Which numbers should be used to estimate 993 + 61?

Ⓐ 1000 + 60
Ⓑ 1000 + 70
Ⓒ 900 + 60
Ⓓ 900 + 70

4. Which is the closest estimate of $13.22 − $5.96?

Ⓐ $5
Ⓑ $6
Ⓒ $7
Ⓓ $8

Go On

5.

Which is the closest estimate for the height of this building?

- Ⓐ 40 ft
- Ⓑ 60 ft
- Ⓒ 80 ft
- Ⓓ 100 ft

6. 31 + 88 is –

- Ⓐ less than 80
- Ⓑ between 80 and 90
- Ⓒ between 90 and 100
- Ⓓ between 100 and 120

7. The closest estimate of 17 × 49 is –

- Ⓐ 10
- Ⓑ 100
- Ⓒ 1000
- Ⓓ 10,000

8. The closest estimate of 209 ÷ 5 is –

- Ⓐ 4
- Ⓑ 40
- Ⓒ 400
- Ⓓ 4000

9.

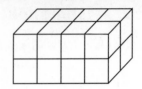

Which is the closest estimate of how many blocks would be needed to make 12 of these figures?

- Ⓐ 100
- Ⓑ 150
- Ⓒ 200
- Ⓓ 250

10. 374 – 68 is –

- Ⓐ less than 200
- Ⓑ between 200 and 250
- Ⓒ between 250 and 300
- Ⓓ more than 300

11. 1200 ÷ 11 is closest to –

- Ⓐ 12
- Ⓑ 120
- Ⓒ 1200
- Ⓓ 12,000

12. $8.92 – $2.04 is closest to –

- Ⓐ $6
- Ⓑ $7
- Ⓒ $8
- Ⓓ $10

Stop

Name _____

PRACTICE 8 • Interpreting Data

SAMPLES

Directions: Harry made this tally chart showing how many cars of each color he saw on his way to school one day. Use the chart to answer the questions.

Color	Number of Cars
Red	IIII
Black	THH IIII
Blue	THH THH II
Green	II
White	THH III

A. How many white cars did Harry see?

Ⓐ 15   Ⓒ 8

Ⓑ 10   Ⓓ 3

B. What color car did he see most often?

Ⓐ Red   Ⓒ Blue

Ⓑ Black   Ⓓ White

Tips and Reminders

• Study the graph or chart carefully. Use it to answer each question.

• After choosing an answer, read the question again to make sure you have answered it correctly.

PRACTICE

Directions: Josie made a chart showing the number of different animals she saw at the seashore. Use the chart to answer questions 1–3.

Animals	Number Seen
Seagulls	23
Mussels	14
Crabs	8
Turtles	1
Snails	5

1. How many crabs did Josie see?

Ⓐ 14   Ⓒ 5

Ⓑ 8   Ⓓ 1

2. What animal did Josie see least?

Ⓐ Mussels   Ⓒ Turtles

Ⓑ Crabs   Ⓓ Snails

3. How many more seagulls than snails did Josie see?

Ⓐ 23   Ⓒ 15

Ⓑ 18   Ⓓ 9

Go On

Directions: Alyssa and her family went on a hiking trip. Alyssa kept track of the number of miles they hiked each day. She put the results in a bar graph. Use the graph to answer questions 4–6.

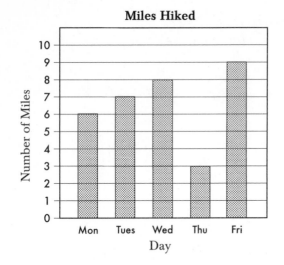

Miles Hiked

4. On which day did Alyssa's family hike exactly 8 miles?

Ⓐ Monday   Ⓒ Wednesday

Ⓑ Tuesday   Ⓓ Thursday

5. On which day did Alyssa's family hike exactly 3 more miles than on Thursday?

Ⓐ Monday   Ⓒ Wednesday

Ⓑ Tuesday   Ⓓ Friday

6. How many miles did Alyssa's family hike on Monday and Tuesday together?

Ⓐ 14   Ⓒ 9

Ⓑ 13   Ⓓ 8

Directions: Daniel made this table to show the number of goals and assists he and his friends had during the hockey season. Use the table to answer questions 7–9.

Goals and Assists

Player	Goals	Assists
Daniel	14	11
Mark	24	5
James	8	4
Peter	12	14
Sam	10	9

7. How many goals and assists did Peter have all together?

Ⓐ 19   Ⓒ 26

Ⓑ 25   Ⓓ 29

8. Mark scored exactly 2 times as many goals as –

Ⓐ Daniel   Ⓒ Peter

Ⓑ James   Ⓓ Sam

9. How many more goals and assists did Daniel have than James ?

Ⓐ 12   Ⓒ 19

Ⓑ 13   Ⓓ 25

Go On

Directions: Lydia made this tally chart showing how many times she did each chore last week. Use the chart to answer questions 10–12.

Chore	Number of Times Done
Wash dishes	┼┼┼ ┼┼┼ ‖
Make bed	┼┼┼ ‖‖
Feed dog	┼┼┼ ┼┼┼ ┼┼┼ │
Sweep floor	‖‖
Take out trash	‖

10. Which chore did Lydia do most often?

(A) Wash dishes (C) Feed dog
(B) Make bed (D) Sweep floor

11. How many times did Lydia wash dishes?

(A) 2 (C) 12
(B) 9 (D) 16

12. Which chore did Lydia do exactly 4 times?

(A) Wash dishes (C) Feed dog
(B) Make bed (D) Sweep floor

Directions: Katy and her friends kept track of the time it took each of them to run one mile. Katy put the results in a bar graph. Use the graph to answer questions 13–15.

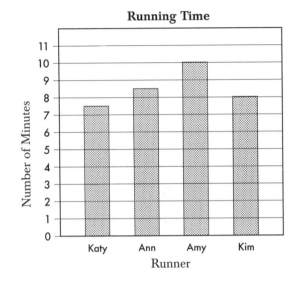

13. Who ran the mile in 8.5 minutes?

(A) Katy (C) Kim
(B) Ann (D) Amy

14. Who took the longest time to run the mile?

(A) Ann (C) Kim
(B) Amy (D) Katy

15. How long did it take Katy to run one mile?

(A) 7.5 minutes (C) 8.5 minutes
(B) 8 minutes (D) 9.5 minutes

Go On

Directions: Bryan asked the members of his family to weigh themselves. He put the results in a table. Use the table to answer questions 16–18.

Family Weights

Name	Weight (Pounds)
Mom	126
Dad	189
Alan	63
Erin	45
Bryan	78

16. Who weighs the least?

- Ⓐ Dad
- Ⓑ Alan
- Ⓒ Erin
- Ⓓ Bryan

17. Who weighs exactly 2 times as much as Alan?

- Ⓐ Mom
- Ⓑ Dad
- Ⓒ Erin
- Ⓓ Bryan

18. How much more does Dad weigh than Bryan?

- Ⓐ 78 lb
- Ⓑ 91 lb
- Ⓒ 101 lb
- Ⓓ 111 lb

Directions: Charlene made a chart showing the number of different state license plates she saw on cars in her town. Use the chart to answer questions 19–20.

State License Plate	Number of Times Seen
Maine	7
New York	23
Vermont	58
New Jersey	17
Massachusetts	46

19. How many times did Charlene see license plates from Vermont?

- Ⓐ 17
- Ⓑ 23
- Ⓒ 46
- Ⓓ 58

20. How many more license plates from Massachusetts did Charlene see than license plates from Maine?

- Ⓐ 39
- Ⓑ 41
- Ⓒ 46
- Ⓓ 51

Stop

Name _____

PRACTICE 9 • Solving Problems

Directions: Choose the best answer to each question.

SAMPLES

A. Marcus had 44 books in his collection. He bought 5 more books. Which question could you answer using this information?

- (A) How much did the books cost?
- (B) How much change did he get?
- (C) How many books does he have in all?
- (D) How many books fit in Marcus's bookcase?

B. Jeannie bought 8 packs of baseball cards. Each pack had 5 cards. Which number sentence should you use to find how many cards she bought in all?

- (A) $8 - 5 = \square$
- (B) $8 \times 5 = \square$
- (C) $8 + 5 = \square$
- (D) $8 \div 5 = \square$

Tips and Reminders

- Underline or jot down important information.
- Check each answer choice. Find the one that has all the information you need.
- Draw a picture if it helps y.ou answer the question.
- Use rounding to estimate the solution to a problem.

PRACTICE

1. Keisha scored 32 goals in field hockey last season. This season she scored 41. Which number sentence should you use to find how many more goals she scored this season?

- (A) $32 + 41 = \square$
- (B) $41 \div 32 = \square$
- (C) $32 \times 41 = \square$
- (D) $41 - 32 = \square$

2. Barry bought a cap for $8.95. He gave the clerk $10.00. Which question could you answer using this information?

- (A) How much change should he receive?
- (B) How long was he at the store?
- (C) How old is Barry?
- (D) What kind of cap did he buy?

Go On

3. Tilly's puppy weighed 6 pounds. Now he weighs 4 times as much. Which number sentence should you use to find how much the puppy weighs now?

(A) $4 \times 6 = \square$

(B) $4 + 6 = \square$

(C) $6 - 4 = \square$

(D) $6 \div 4 = \square$

4. Canute started a game with $500. Two hours later, he had $150 left. Which number sentence shows how much money he lost?

(A) $\$500 \times \$150 = \square$

(B) $\$500 + \$150 = \square$

(C) $\$500 - \$150 = \square$

(D) $\$500 \div \$150 = \square$

5. The Caseys bought 12 ears of corn for dinner and shared them equally. What else do you need to know to find how many ears of corn each member of the family had?

(A) how much the 12 ears of corn cost

(B) the number of people in the family

(C) how long it took to cook the corn

(D) the time it took to finish dinner

6. Jerry saved $19.40 per week for 6 weeks. <u>About</u> how much did he save in all?

(A) $100

(B) $120

(C) $140

(D) $160

7. At 4:00 P.M., there were 9 children at the park. At 5:00 P.M., there were 3 times as many children. Which number sentence shows how many children were there at 5:00 P.M.?

(A) $5 \times 9 = \square$

(B) $5 + 9 = \square$

(C) $9 - 3 = \square$

(D) $9 \times 3 = \square$

8. There are 120 seats in a movie theater. At the 7:00 P.M. show, there were 42 empty seats. Which question could you answer using this information?

(A) What movie did people see?

(B) How many people went to the 7:00 P.M. show?

(C) How long did the movie last?

(D) How many people enjoyed the show and how many did not?

9. In a basketball game, 4 players scored a total of 97 points. <u>About</u> how many points did each player score?

(A) 20

(B) 25

(C) 30

(D) 35

10. Gwen spent $38.99 for a jacket and $18.95 for sneakers. <u>About</u> how much did she spend in all?

(A) $40

(B) $50

(C) $60

(D) $70

11. Claire worked for 15 hours last week. She earned $5.25 per hour. Which number sentence should you use to find how much she earned in all?

Ⓐ $15 - \$5.25 = \square$

Ⓑ $\$5.25 + 15 = \square$

Ⓒ $\$5.25 \div 15 = \square$

Ⓓ $15 \times \$5.25 = \square$

12. A total of 320 cars went through the car wash on Saturday. What information do you need to find how many cars were washed per hour?

Ⓐ how many hours the car wash was open

Ⓑ what kinds of cars went through the car wash

Ⓒ how much the car wash charges for each car

Ⓓ how many people worked at the car wash on Saturday

13. Ms. Walker took in $840 at her hardware store on Tuesday. She paid her 4 workers a total of $160 for the day. Which number sentence shows how much money she had left over?

Ⓐ $\$840 + \$160 = \square$

Ⓑ $\$840 - \$160 = \square$

Ⓒ $\$840 \div \$160 = \square$

Ⓓ $\$160 \div 4 = \square$

14. Marilu has $12.00. She wants to buy some 32-cent stamps. Which number sentence shows how to find the number of 32-cent stamps she could buy?

Ⓐ $\$12.00 - \$0.32 = \square$

Ⓑ $\$0.32 + \square = \$12.00$

Ⓒ $\$12.00 \div \$0.32 = \square$

Ⓓ $\$12.00 \times \$0.32 = \square$

15. Mick scored 190 points in his first game of darts, 155 points in his second game, and 205 points in his third game. Which numbers would give you the closest estimate of how many points he scored in all?

Ⓐ $200 + 200 + 200$

Ⓑ $150 + 150 + 200$

Ⓒ $200 + 100 + 200$

Ⓓ $200 + 150 + 200$

16. Calvin put 12 golf balls in each of 5 bags and had 6 left over. Which number sentence shows how many golf balls Calvin had in all?

Ⓐ $12 + 5 + 6 = \square$

Ⓑ $(12 \times 5) + 6 = \square$

Ⓒ $(12 \div 5) + 6 = \square$

Ⓓ $(12 \times 5) \times 6 = \square$

Stop

Name _____

PRACTICE 10 • Word Problems

Directions: Solve each problem.

SAMPLES

A. Lucy bought some gift wrap for $2.99 and a card for $1.25. How much change should she get back from a 5-dollar bill?

Ⓐ $4.24   Ⓒ $0.76

Ⓑ $2.01   Ⓓ $0.66

B. Brad is making pumpkin bread. He needs 2 cups of whole wheat flour and 1 cup of white flour. If 1 cup = 8 ounces, how many ounces of flour does he need in all?

Ⓐ 16 ounces

Ⓑ 24 ounces

Ⓒ 32 ounces

Ⓓ 48 ounces

Tips and Reminders

• Underline or jot down important information to help you answer each question.

• Write a number sentence to help find the answer.

• Draw a picture if it will help you solve the problem.

• If you have trouble solving the problem, try each answer choice to see which one works.

PRACTICE

1. Allison used to run the race course in a minute and a half. Now she can run it in 20 seconds less. How long does it take Allison to run the course now?

Ⓐ 50 seconds

Ⓑ 60 seconds

Ⓒ 70 seconds

Ⓓ 90 seconds

2. Ramon bought 3 pounds of nails for $5.96 and some tape for $1.79. How much did Ramon spend in all?

Ⓐ $4.17

Ⓑ $6.65

Ⓒ $6.75

Ⓓ $7.75

Go On

3. The owner of a farmstand sold 18 bags of potatoes. Each bag weighed 8 pounds. How many pounds of potatoes were sold in all?

Ⓐ 26 lb   Ⓒ 136 lb

Ⓑ 84 lb   Ⓓ 144 lb

4. It takes Moira twice as long to mow the lawn as it does for her to water the garden. She can do both jobs in 45 minutes. How long does it take her to water the garden?

Ⓐ 15 minutes

Ⓑ 30 minutes

Ⓒ 45 minutes

Ⓓ 60 minutes

5. Lou put 125 olives in 4 jars as equally as possible. <u>About</u> how many olives did he put in each jar?

Ⓐ 25   Ⓒ 35

Ⓑ 30   Ⓓ 40

6. Four girls are standing in a line. Jenny is standing directly behind Pam. Sal is ahead of Pam and behind Colleen. Who is last in line?

Ⓐ Jenny

Ⓑ Pam

Ⓒ Sal

Ⓓ Colleen

7. Jade has a basket full of buttons. The chart below shows how many of each color she has.

Color of Button	Number of Buttons
Silver	24
Gold	43
Black	35
White	29

If Jade reaches into the basket and takes one button without looking, which color is she most likely to pick?

Ⓐ silver   Ⓒ black

Ⓑ gold   Ⓓ white

8. Mr. Fong makes 12 wood carvings per week in his crafts shop. At this rate, how many carvings will he make in 8 weeks?

Ⓐ 20   Ⓒ 96

Ⓑ 48   Ⓓ 128

9. Nita is playing a game with the spinner shown below. If she spins the spinner 30 times, how many times is the spinner likely to land on 3?

Ⓐ 6 times   Ⓒ 12 times

Ⓑ 10 times   Ⓓ 15 times

10. T-shirts are on sale at 3 for $12.00. At this price, how much would 5 T-shirts cost?

   Ⓐ $15.00   Ⓒ $20.00
   Ⓑ $18.00   Ⓓ $22.00

11. A stone wall is 4 yards and 2 feet long. How many feet long is the wall?

   Ⓐ 10 ft   Ⓒ 16 ft
   Ⓑ 14 ft   Ⓓ 18 ft

12. Mr. Price drove 185 kilometers on Monday and 234 kilometers on Tuesday. How many more kilometers did he drive on Tuesday than on Monday?

   Ⓐ 49   Ⓒ 149
   Ⓑ 51   Ⓓ 419

13. Two scout troops collected aluminum cans. Troop 1 collected 72 cans. Troop 2 collected twice as many. How many cans did the two troops collect in all?

   Ⓐ 144   Ⓒ 216
   Ⓑ 180   Ⓓ 288

14. Garth wants to buy some 32-cent stamps. How many stamps can he buy for $19.20?

   Ⓐ 40   Ⓒ 60
   Ⓑ 50   Ⓓ 70

Kelly plans to go mountain biking on Saturday. The sign below shows the trails she can take. Use this information to answer questions 15–16.

Trail	Distance
Mud City	6.1 mi
River Bend	4.3 mi
Tom's Peak	2.8 mi
Hunger Road	7.5 mi

15. How many miles would Kelly ride if she rode all four trails?

   Ⓐ 10.4 miles
   Ⓑ 13.2 miles
   Ⓒ 19.7 miles
   Ⓓ 20.7 miles

16. How much longer is the Hunger Road trail than the Tom's Peak trail?

   Ⓐ 4.7 miles
   Ⓑ 3.7 miles
   Ⓒ 3.2 miles
   Ⓓ 1.4 miles

17. Alan started his homework at 3:30 P.M. He finished at 6:20 P.M. How long did it take him to do his homework?

   Ⓐ 3 hours 50 minutes
   Ⓑ 3 hours 40 minutes
   Ⓒ 2 hours 50 minutes
   Ⓓ 2 hours 40 minutes

Go On

18. Larry is 4 ft 2 in. tall. Cam is 3 inches taller than Larry but 2 inches shorter than Mike. How tall is Mike?

Ⓐ 4 ft 5 in.

Ⓑ 4 ft 7 in.

Ⓒ 4 ft 9 in.

Ⓓ 5 ft

19. Four tickets for the baseball game cost a total of $88.00. If each ticket costs the same, what is the price of 1 ticket?

Ⓐ $44.00

Ⓑ $31.00

Ⓒ $24.00

Ⓓ $22.00

20. A machine makes 32 computer disks per hour. At this rate, about how many disks will the machine make in 9 hours?

Ⓐ 200   Ⓒ 400

Ⓑ 300   Ⓓ 500

21. In 3 different weeks, Maggie earned $185, $305, and $290. About how much did she earn altogether?

Ⓐ $600   Ⓒ $800

Ⓑ $700   Ⓓ $1000

22. One oil tank holds 175 gallons of oil. Another tank holds 325 gallons. How much more oil does the larger tank hold?

Ⓐ 125 gallons

Ⓑ 150 gallons

Ⓒ 175 gallons

Ⓓ 250 gallons

23. Raffle tickets cost $2.00 each or 6 for $10.00. How much would it cost to buy a total of 15 raffle tickets?

Ⓐ $20.00

Ⓑ $24.00

Ⓒ $26.00

Ⓓ $30.00

24. Marla has 33 party favors. How many friends can get party favors if she gives 3 to each person?

Ⓐ 10   Ⓒ 12

Ⓑ 11   Ⓓ 13

25. Crow's Car Lot has 23 blue cars, 35 white cars, and 16 black cars. There are 125 cars on the lot in all. How many cars of other colors are there?

Ⓐ 51   Ⓒ 74

Ⓑ 67   Ⓓ 80

Stop